About Dying

Advance Reviews

"As a medical doctor, Colin Dicks is well qualified to write a book with the title, "About Dying."

His appraisal of death and dying, coming from his own personal observations and interactions, provides an honest approach to a most difficult subject.

As this book carefully explores issues surrounding death and dying, it provides great encouragement to live well - to live with hope."

Paul Lanham – Pastor
Flametree Church, Nambour, Australia.

"This compassionate and insightful handbook assists people living in the face of death to move beyond fear and silence. It provides gentle guidance and reassurance to support the emotional, interpersonal and spiritual healing that enables people to live, die and grieve well."

Odette Waanders - CEO
Palliative Care Victoria, Australia.

"Dr. Dicks succeeds in offering us a candid and fresh perspective of death as a natural and hope-filled process. While sharing his Christian perspective of hope, Dr. Dicks invites the readers to welcome this reality as an opportunity to live more fully and intentionally. This book *is a timely and valuable resource for those terminally ill and those who care for them -family, friends and medical professionals alike. "*

Monique Cerundolo, MA, BCC

Losing a parent is a difficult and challenging time. Finding out your parent is dying from cancer can fuel emotions of uncertainty and helplessness. As I'm facing this challenge I've found Dr Colin Dicks and his book "About Dying" has the answers to many of my questions. Simply written, I've found "About Dying" an excellent resource for my parents and myself to navigate the way through the emotional roller coaster that we all need to face at some point in our lives. Thank you Dr Dicks for making our journey easier.

Sharon Cooper
Published Author, Business Owner

Your book touched, not just on the focus of people facing death, but considered loved ones and the professional caregivers as well. I felt comforted in both my work and on a personal level. You offered affirmation to some things I have considered and more than I had hoped for in covering areas in such a sensitive topic.

'About Dying' is an extraordinary book that touches on all we could hope for personally and professionally.

Carol Fleer , R.N

About Dying

How to live in the face of death

Dr. Colin Dicks

First Edition

About Dying
How to live in the face of death

ISBN (Trade Paperback)   978-0-9924545-0-0
ISBN (.mobi eBook)   978-0-9924545-1-7
ISBN (.epub eBook)   978-0-9924545-2-4

www.dyingtounderstand.com

First Edition

*I dedicate this book to those
who have travelled this road before me
and to those who will follow on behind.*

Contents

Foreword

Here is a bold attempt to define the path where no mortal man has gone before and be able to tell the story. It is a giant step, but one that has been worthwhile. Colin points out that "there are no professionals when it comes to dying. Each one has to travel the path once and alone". It is a book about "how to live facing death".

This is a book for those who have heard the dreadful prognosis that their time on earth is limited, even if that amount of time cannot be quantified. The anguish of not knowing how long or how painful, if at all, can make this journey an extremely difficult one. This volume gives you the "Hitchhikers Guide" to the journey through the eyes of one who has seen countless lives, touched by the "tap on the shoulder" that we all fear and no one wants to receive. The tap, once received, cannot be taken back, unlike the games you play as a child.

This is the workbook for the test you never wanted to take. It is the crib sheet for those who want to get an understanding of the subject. You can't cheat on this test and no one else can take it for you. You have to do it yourself, but as Colin elaborates, it is one test that everyone passes. There are no honour grades, and no one fails. But, if you want to go in to the test prepared, this is the book for you. It helps explain many of the issues and problems we will all face on the way.

Colin covers the many spiritual approaches of the world's faiths which may help those adherents to face the uncertain future with a little more comfort. The non-believers will not have as much to support them in their journey, but a frank discussion of the issues as given by Colin should show them a path and help to reduce anxiety somewhat. The discussion of near death experiences, which happen to "believers" and "non-believers" alike, may be of some comfort. Colin has his own spiritual walk, and I am pleased to see that he has not pushed his beliefs on his readers. It is a book for those of faith and for those of no faith.

Shakespeare said, in Julius Caesar, that the "coward dies a thousand deaths, the brave die but once". It is easy to put yourself in the coward category if you have no knowledge, but with information in this book, you will be able to be" brave" in the face of it. I have often said to my patients who have a terminal illness that if they retreat and shake in their boots, that they will miss the opportunity to interact with their loved ones, and the period of waiting will seem eternal misery. By facing it full on, they will enjoy the comfort of their loved ones and will often be the one who helps bring the comforters some comfort of their own. It will be a life well lived.

I recommend this book for all those who are facing their own mortality, for those who work with them, and for those who will inevitably walk the same path at some stage. Being forewarned is being forearmed. As someone who has spent the better part of 40 years dealing with young haematology patients, older patients in solid tumour medical oncology and as a palliative care physician, I wish I had had this resource available years ago.

Dr Geoffrey Hawson
Associate Professor (University of Queensland)
MBBS; FRACP; FAChPM; FRCPA (1976)
Haematology Oncology Palliative Services

Preface

As an oncologist, I work with death and dying. Not everyone diagnosed with cancer will be cured. Consequently, I often find myself in the position of having to break the bad news to patients that the condition is terminal.

I cannot imagine how difficult it must be to be told that there is no cure and that, in all probability, life will end as a result of cancer. I see the range of emotion my patients go through: the shock, the anger and the denial. I share their feelings of loss. I often have little to say in these trying circumstances; rather, I just try to be there for the many brave people who have to face the reality of dying.

But this is only the beginning of the journey. After that fateful first or perhaps second consultation, life goes on for many patients. The dreaded news has been delivered as if this absolves doctors from further responsibility. It is as if, once the bad news has been broken, there is no further need for care. But this is when care is most needed, when hearts are broken, and loss and grief are so real.

Try to start a conversation about death and dying and you will find out how brief the exchange can be. For many people who find themselves in conversation with someone who is dying, often the easiest (and most comfortable) option is to offer a platitude of sorts and swiftly change the subject. This is simply not good enough.

My perception of the great need to address the difficult subject of death and dying and to offer a real discussion about the key issues drove me to write this book. It has taken many rewrites and years to finalise the essence of what I think is important. But then again, I am only an observer until my time to die arrives. I am sure my outlook may change.

This book is for those facing a terminal illness. It offers an opportunity to face death with an element of hope and the courage to believe that things will turn out just fine. It is a resource for carers who often struggle to understand the difficulty of the journey ahead.

There are no professionals when it comes to dying. Each one has to travel the path once and alone. This book is a companion to make the journey a little less daunting. It is a rough map of the journey ahead. It is a resource that we all may inevitably need as we complete this adventure of life.

Death is a natural end to life. It comes to us all. Sharing the experience makes the journey easier. I trust that you will have a safe journey and that you will find comfort in the information in the book.

Acknowledgments

Many people have contributed to this book. Each person has provided the spark of inspiration and belief that has kept me writing and allowed me to learn. Without their contribution *About Dying* would be no more than an unfulfilled dream.

My heartfelt thanks go to my wife, Mathilde, who has been a constant source of encouragement. She has kept my writing dream alive. My children, Matthew, Jessica, Abigail and Joshua, should also be acknowledged for putting up with the 'next draft' of the manuscript over the years.

My thanks go to Kirsty Racher for being an outstanding editor who keeps my writing honest and relevant. I'd also like to thank Daniel Barrozo for transforming my manuscript into a book and for providing invaluable advice about publishing.

I am most grateful to the following people for their contribution: Danna Rankin for her enthusiasm about all of my projects and Sharon Cooper for her advice about writing, speaking and publishing.

A final thank you to the countless friends and family members who have had to listen to yet another episode of my book saga. It is finally finished!

Introduction

I have seen death many times. It sometimes arrives quickly and unexpectedly, as it snatches away life in a moment of confusion and terror. These deaths are traumatic and unfair and there is little time to be prepared for the unforeseen tragedy.

But death is not always cruel. It is sometimes a kind end to a world of suffering. It is sometimes the gentle end to a life well lived as it carefully carries the aged and frail away in their sleep. Death is not the enemy when it frees those trapped in the prison of dementia, or relieves those with intractable cancer pain from their suffering.

Death has been given a bad name. We are led to believe that it may never happen to us, but the reality is that we all have to die. Death is a certainty and there are two ways to approach this natural event. The first is to avoid the topic altogether, pretending our death will never happen and fighting against it when it occurs. The second is to understand what happens when death arrives, to be prepared for the event and, as far as possible, accept the reality of death.

As a doctor, I have witnessed many deaths. Two stand out in in particular. The first was the death of Mrs Blades. She had terminal cancer and had been told she had only days to live. She responded to this news with complete peace and tranquillity. Given her limited prognosis and desire to be alone, Mrs Blades was tucked away in a small side-room of the hospital away from other patients. She was frail and ill, yet she was never without a smile and a friendly word. Her husband, her trusty companion, sat beside her, and together they celebrated her life. There was no bemoaning their loss, or expressions of sorrow or pity, but rather an excitement and an expectation of a life to come based on their faith. They had a view of eternity, one that promised paradise after dying. Mrs Blades was ready to die. She did so in peace, even through the struggle of dying.

Julie, in contrast, was diagnosed with an incurable cancer. She was determined to fight it and beat it, but this was not to be. As her disease progressed, Julie remained in denial. She refused to accept the fact that she was dying. Because of this, Julie's death was traumatic as she defended herself against the reality of her mortality. She did not have a good death.

Over the years, I have seen people hold on to life, clutch at it in desperation in a fierce battle that invariably is lost. Death cannot be defeated. I have seen others let go and allow death to occur. They have made their peace, they have said their goodbyes and they are ready.

Being prepared for death is a gloomy topic. The subject of one's own death is one most people prefer to avoid. Perhaps if we look away, close our ears and our eyes and stop our thoughts from turning towards death, it won't happen to us. Nothing could be further from the truth. Being ready for death allows the event to occur in the best possible way. We can prepare ourselves, in practical, emotional and spiritual terms, for the fact that we will die. We can make peace and enjoy the time we have left with loved ones. We can live the life we have left to us on this earth. Knowing where death leads and being able to die with confidence is a remarkable gift. This gift is available to all, but it does require some preparation.

Preparing for death is a challenging journey. It requires courage, an open mind and time. Take the time to understand this thing called death and the process of dying. It may not be as terrible as you imagine.

Chapter 1: Everyday Death

I am not afraid of death; I just don't want
to be there when it happens.
– Woody Allen

It is surprising how much death surrounds us if we care to look. In fact, we are often perpetrators of death, delighting ourselves in the untimely demise of unwanted houseguests such as wasps or termites. Personally, I don't particularly mind seeing the end of flies, mosquitoes or spiders. Snakes would also be on my unwanted list, but the law protects them from extermination. No person has made it to the list so far, although there have been a few close calls.

We often cause death without even thinking about it. When I drive home at night, I am responsible for the death of hundreds of bugs who are unfortunate enough to find themselves in the way of my windshield; I pause only to curse their splattered remnants the next day. Who has ever been distraught at the death of a pumpkin, or the untimely demise of a beetroot? Or offended when potatoes are uprooted?

Death is all around us, and we are unmoved. We understand it to be a natural part of the cycle of life in which living organisms are born, hatched or spawned. They reach maturity, reproduce, briefly exist and then die. These organisms decay, returning to the soil or water to be recycled as organic matter. In nature, we rely on death to ensure the survival of the species. It is an essential filter, removing the old and making room for the new.

DEATH AT A DISTANCE IS QUITE ACCEPTABLE TO US. IT ONLY BECOMES UNACCEPTABLE WHEN IT BECOMES PERSONAL.

At some level, we can also accept that death is part of human life. For example, we may recognise it as a release from suffering for those who are old and frail. There are constant reminders of death in our society – the cemeteries with lonely tombstones that we drive past, giving those resting there little thought, the funerals we attend and the daily news reports blaring out from our television screens. There is overwhelming evidence that death is part of everyday life.

Death at a distance is quite acceptable to us. It only becomes unacceptable when it becomes personal. When death affects us directly, we sit up and take notice. When it looks in our direction, or in the direction of someone we love, we object loudly. We fear and suffer the loss associated with everyday death.

Over time, we have learnt to cope with death, establishing rituals, such as funerals, to allow us to make sense of this seemingly senseless event. A century ago, death was commonplace, taking the young as well as the old. Children died of diseases we can no longer pronounce or even recognise. In the United States of America, only four people in every hundred made it to the age of sixty-five in the early 1900s. People died at home, and it was the family's responsibility to administer the death rituals in order to close the chapter and move on. Death was an everyday topic and part of normal life.

Over time, our society has become one in which death has become almost obscene. The whole process of dying has been sanitised, sterilised and removed from the home. Dying people are whisked away to hospital where strangers in the guise of medical professionals attend to them. Post-mortem, those who have died are transported to distant buildings and nameless places. The final farewell is a thirty-minute, blitz-cremation ceremony, and then it is all over. Instant coffee, instant funeral!

THE ILLUSION HAS BEEN CREATED THAT WE DON'T HAVE TO DIE. THE EXPECTATION IS THAT DYING IS STRICTLY FORBIDDEN.

It is little wonder death has become so distressing in the modern world. The illusion has been created that we don't have to die. The expectation is that dying is strictly forbidden. Death has become an unmentionable event. It has been portrayed as the worst of all possible things, leaving terror and fear in its wake. These sentiments are not necessarily true if death is put into perspective and recognised and respected as a normal part of everyday life.

Consider the following statements about death.

Death is a natural event

Usually, death is the end result of ageing although it may arrive a little sooner as a result of neglect or accident. Too much alcohol, too many cigarettes or insufficient exercise may hasten our demise. Accidents and tragedies happen along the path of life. They are out of our hands and we have no control over the circumstances that end life unexpectedly. Generally speaking, dying is the perfectly natural end to a long life.

Death is an unavoidable event

Leaping off mountains with or without parachutes, swimming with sharks or driving at speed while saturated with alcohol are all ways of loudly attracting the unwanted attention of death. Many of us, however, live our lives in an effort to deter death – we exercise vigorously, pop our multivitamins, antioxidants and fish-oil capsules, and eat healthily. Even with our best efforts, however, death cannot be avoided forever.

Death is an everyday event

About 150,000 people died yesterday; tomorrow will see a similar tally and today will be no exception. Death is an everyday event, particularly if we consider the biosphere of all living matter in which billions of organisms perish daily. Those organisms now living are far fewer in number than those who have lived.

Death unites us

By this, I mean there are no exceptions. Death will come to us all. The rich are not exempt, nor the famous, the poor or religious. Kings and queens are not excluded, and neither are movie stars. It happens to the best of us and the worst of us. The rule that applies to all living things is, "If you were born, then so you must die."

Death is an acceptable event

Many people would disagree with this statement, but the truth is, it has to be. We can't avoid, deny, postpone or outwit death. When faced with its reality, we have two choices. The first is to deny death and be surprised when it happens. The other is to accept death and be prepared when it happens. Regardless of the choice we make, our death will eventually occur. Accepting death is the challenge for all of us.

> OUR DEATH WILL EVENTUALLY OCCUR. ACCEPTING DEATH IS THE CHALLENGE FOR ALL OF US.

Chapter 2: The Process of Ageing

Death is caused by swallowing small amounts
of saliva over a long period of time.
Attributed to George Carlin

Birth and death are at opposite ends of life, and the action that connects them is the troublesome process of ageing. Ageing, or senescence, can be defined as a loss of function over time.

We start life with the dramatic event of birth. If this is anything to go by, life is always going to be an adventure! In childhood, each new life stage is marked and rejoiced in. Perhaps you can recall the joy of a toddler taking the first faltering steps, or a baby smiling and flashing those fabulous two front teeth. We celebrate birthdays, decorate cakes and take delight in the amazing growth and development of our children. The grandest celebration occurs when a person reaches the age of twenty-one. Champagne corks pop as we recognise this as the coming of age.

Once we have reached adulthood, the years quickly accrue. Counted still in single units in our twenties, the years become ever more blurred and merged into each other in our thirties. By the time we get to our fifties, age is counted in leap years. We celebrate (or mourn) significant birthday milestones of sixty, seventy or eighty years. Although it remains constant, plodding on at a steady twenty-four hours in a day, we begin to feel that time is racing along. Conversely, physically we slow down as we are affected by the functional decline that comes with age.

NOTHING REMAINS NEW FOREVER, AND THIS IS PARTICULARLY SO WITH OUR FRAGILE BIOLOGICAL SYSTEM.

Living is rather like a train journey: the train relentlessly moves from one station to the next until it is at last no longer able to function or capable of repair. What starts off as a shiny new locomotive eventually ends up as rusty old scrap metal.

The same principle of wear and tear applies to most things. Clothes become threadbare, shoes wear out, equipment malfunctions, and even the seemingly permanent features of the landscape change. Nothing remains new forever, and this is particularly so with our fragile biological system.

At the most basic level, our existence is determined by the billions of cells that form our tissues, organs and body. Some of these cells don't last very long before they become worn out and die. The body must constantly renew cells and replace dead cells to sustain life. Skin cells, for example, last for about two weeks before they die and flake off to contribute as dust on the mantelpiece. The cells lining the intestine are replaced every few weeks. We don't notice these small and frequent deaths occurring on and inside us as new cells replace the worn out ones.

WITH TIME, MORE AND MORE ERRORS ACCUMULATE IN OUR GENETIC CODE AND THE CELLULAR PROCESSES BEGIN TO MALFUNCTION.

This fine balance of degeneration and regeneration is beautifully controlled by our amazing genetic code. Genes provide the blueprint for cellular activity, sending exact messages about how cells must function. They determine the colour of our eyes, the length of our arms, our IQ, height and, probably, weight. Our genes are a gift, determining our talents as well as our limitations. In a sense, they also determine how long we will live.

As with all things, genes are not immune to the process of ageing. They too require ongoing maintenance and repair, and will eventually deteriorate. With time, more and more errors accumulate in our genetic code and the cellular processes begin to malfunction. Cells fail to adequately perform, resulting in degeneration and illness. Kidney cells are unable to filter urine adequately, resulting in renal failure. Brain cells are unable to transmit information as effectively, resulting in dementia. Cartilage cells are unable to be replaced, resulting in arthritis. We become old and frail with time.

Reaching the peak of health at the age of twenty, we spend much of our adulthood fighting against getting old. We spend hundreds of dollars on attempts to arrest the evidence of ageing – the use of multivitamins, cosmetic surgery, facial creams and little blue pills all testify to this battle. Unfortunately, it's a battle we are destined to lose. Over time, we will lose our hearing and flexibility. Our toes will become out of reach. Our muscle mass and bone mass will reduce, and our metabolic rates decline. Both our mental function and sexual function deteriorate. Body parts start to sag and droop, and degenerative conditions such as arthritis, dementia and cancer become common. We become weaker, bulkier and shorter. We surprisingly become more and more like our parents.

IT IS BETTER TO GROW OLD THAN TO DIE YOUNG YET THE PROCESS OF AGEING IS ASSOCIATED WITH LOSS.

It is better to grow old than to die young yet the process of ageing is associated with loss. There is the loss of confidence and independence. Many of the abilities we took for granted, such as being able to drive and maintain a licence, are lost. We lose vitality and energy and become unable to do the most basic of tasks. Friends are lost as they pass on. Being ninety is a very lonely and difficult age. Living to a very old age is not without its limitations. At this stage in life, death is not necessarily an enemy.

We know that life cannot continue forever. Few of us want to live forever. As we age we hope to retain the liberties of youth for as long as possible. Our memories serve us well, recalling the good times more often than the bad. As we age we may lose our physical ability but we can share our wisdom. We have an opportunity to leave the example of our life as a legacy for others. To my mind, it is neither the beginning nor the end that matters as much as how we choose to live our lives.

Chapter 3: Defining Death

*No drowning man can know which drop
of water his last breath did stop...*
– Sir Charles Sedley-To Cloris

W e know that death is irreversible and final. As a young boy, I learnt this fundamental rule playing "cops and robbers". When you were shot with an imaginary bullet, you died. Huge arguments raged about the validity of the shot. "You missed!" or "It was only a graze!" were assertions we frequently bawled at each other during our games. We tried any means of persuasion to convince our playmates that we were not dead because we all understood the rule that being dead meant "Game over!" Being dead was an absolute; death had no degrees to it.

In reality, however, there is a transitional phase between being alive and being dead. While there's an argument that we (physiologically at least) begin the process of dying from the moment of birth, there is a point at which our impending death becomes apparent. This transition may be instantaneous – death in a plane crash or from a sudden cardiac event usually happens without a great deal of warning, for example. Generally, however, the transition from life to death is slower, and we have a gradual awareness that death is near at hand.

DEATH IS ESTABLISHED BY THE ABSENCE OF A HEARTBEAT, RESPIRATION OR BRAIN ACTIVITY. YET DEFINING THE MOMENT OF DEATH IS NOT NECESSARILY THAT SIMPLE.

It is often impossible to pinpoint the exact moment of death. This was brought home to me when I was working as a junior doctor in a hospital emergency department and met Jacob.

Jacob was brought into the emergency department. No one knew much about this homeless person. He had no friends or relatives. There was no clear medical history. He had the thinness of an advanced illness and was barely conscious. My role was to care for him.

It was clear that Jacob was dying and he was to be left to die in peace. With the understanding that peace, in all senses of the word, is impossible to attain in an emergency department, he was ushered into a smaller, private room. He was connected to an ECG machine recording his heartbeat. His routine observations – blood pressure, pulse rate, consciousness and respiratory rate – were recorded, but no other treatment administered.

Initially, Jacob was partly conscious; he seemed to mutter a few incoherent words and be vaguely aware of his surroundings. He feebly responded to stimuli, but became less responsive as time drew on. Eventually, Jacob could not be roused, and it was clear that he would not react to pain. His basic reflexes, however, continued to display remnants of life. He would have blinked if someone touched his cornea. His pupils obediently constricted in bright light.

As Jacob lapsed deeper into a coma, his breathing became irregular. His heart rate slowed down, misfiring more regularly. The intervals between his breaths increased, with only occasional gasps for air.

At some point Jacob no longer needed air. His pupils remained dilated and no longer responded to light. His ECG tracing was a horizontal flat line.

Jacob was dead.

The passing of Jacob allowed me a unique opportunity to witness the process of dying. I am not sure exactly when he died. From a medical perspective, we take our cues from the cessation of bodily functions. Death is established by the absence of a heartbeat, respiration or brain activity. Yet defining the moment of death is not necessarily that simple.

Consider the remarkable story of Christine Bolden, who suffered a massive brain haemorrhage while being pregnant with twins (CBS Interactive Inc., 2012). Christine was declared brain dead. Using advanced medical technology, however, her body was kept "alive" long enough to allow for the safe delivery of her twins by way of a caesarean section, more than a month after her "death".

The case of Terri Schiavo also illustrates the dilemmas in making apparently simple definitions of life and death. Terri suddenly collapsed in 1990, and as a consequence, ended up in a permanent vegetative state. In 1998, her husband started legal proceedings to stop feeding her. Terri's parents vehemently opposed him. Terri eventually died on 31 March 2005, fifteen years after her collapse. It took the courts seven years to determine whether Terri was dead or alive.

DEFINING THE EXACT MOMENT OF DEATH IS IMPOSSIBLE.

What defines being alive? As we can see from the tragic cases of Christine Bolden and Terri Schiavo, establishing the moment of biological death is not always clear cut. The absence of biological processes that indicate life, such as breathing or a heartbeat, does not necessarily mean that death has occurred. With victims of hypothermia, for example, the frozen and apparently lifeless body has to be warmed and thawed and resuscitated; only then, in the absence of vital signs, can a verdict of death be declared. Medical personnel are sometimes able to resuscitate people who have stopped breathing or whose heart has stopped beating, sometimes after several minutes have gone by. Consider the remarkable event of a cardiac transplant, during which the heart of the patient is physically removed from the body. It is uncanny to see the heart removed with a gaping hole in the patient's chest.

Alive without a heart! The swish and swirl of the artificial circulation machines and hiss of the ventilators are unable to convince me that this is not pure magic.

ALTHOUGH NO ONE CAN BE SURE ABOUT THE EXACT MOMENT OF DEATH, THERE IS COMPELLING EVIDENCE TO SUGGEST THAT A REMARKABLE EVENT OCCURS AT THE TIME OF DEATH. THIS IRREVERSIBLE EVENT IS THOUGHT TO BE THE SEPARATION OF THE SOUL FROM THE BODY.

Defining the exact moment of death is impossible. But it is easy to define the moment *after* death when sustained biological activities are no longer possible. It is apparent that an irreversible event occurs at the moment of death that makes further life unsustainable. Even with the best medical support and care, and the most heroic resuscitation efforts, biological life is impossible once this event has occurred.

Although no one can be sure about the exact moment of death, there is compelling evidence to suggest that a remarkable event occurs at the time of death. This irreversible event is thought to be the separation of the soul from the body. As crazy as it seems, Dr Duncan MacDougall weighed the body at the moment of death and concluded a mass loss of 21 grams. Is this the weight of the soul? The possibility of the soul is worth exploring but physical death must come first.

Chapter 4: Physical Death

Dying is a wild night and a new road.
– Emily Dickinson

We will all die differently. For each of us the circumstances of our death – the surroundings, the timing and the people with us when we die – will be unique. The process of dying, however, is often quite predictable.

Understanding this process is important because it may help to reduce our natural fear and anxiety about dying. When faced with the prospect of death, people commonly want to know: *Will it hurt? Will I suffer? Will I lose my dignity?*

Those who die instantly, in an accident or from a sudden critical event, don't get the chance to ask these questions. Similarly, those who suffer a catastrophic and unexpected major illness or injury, and who subsequently die over several days, are possibly so caught up in the fierce battle for life that they never have an opportunity to consider these questions.

For these people, death arrives unannounced and without warning. These can be difficult deaths for families and friends, who are often left stunned by the sudden event. These people and their families will have no time for goodbyes and no time to prepare, and the tragedy is all the greater for this reason. As well as dealing with the emotional trauma, the families left behind often find themselves enmeshed in the uncertainties of more practical considerations, such as the absence of a last will and testament, or other financial loose ends.

> WHEN FACED WITH THE PROSPECT OF DEATH, PEOPLE COMMONLY WANT TO KNOW: WILL IT HURT? WILL I SUFFER? WILL I LOSE MY DIGNITY?

For the rest of us dying, like birth, is a *perfectly natural* process that progresses over time. Birth sheds light on dying.

The natural process of childbirth

Birth is not instant. It takes forty weeks to progress from conception to the eventual birth. Initially, there are no clues as to the secret little life in the womb. The pregnant mother is an exclusive witness to the first clues as she may experience the hint of nausea in the mornings, or find that her usual monthly period is absent. Gradually, the woman's body undergoes physical changes associated with the pregnancy. Breasts become larger and tender, appetites change and all kinds of weird food may be on the menu.

DYING, LIKE BIRTH, IS A PERFECTLY NATURAL PROCESS THAT PROGRESSES OVER TIME. BIRTH SHEDS LIGHT ON DYING.

As the pregnancy progresses, the signs of new life become more apparent and visible for all to see. As the baby grows in the womb, so the abdomen swells. Little movements turn into vibrant, vigorous kicks. The final few weeks are a waiting game as the start of labour is both eagerly and fearfully anticipated.

Labour is an irreversible and inevitably traumatic set of events for both mother and baby. Labour begins with the onset of uterine contractions, and over a period of hours, the drama of childbirth unfolds. Birth has an uncertain beginning and a definite end.

From the baby's perspective, birth may be even more dramatic. Confined in the warmth and comfort of the womb, this new little person is suddenly subject to intense, squeezing pressure. The pressure is incredible and uncomfortable. The warm, fluid world suddenly disappears and it hurts as powerful contractions force the baby into this new, unfamiliar world of overwhelming light, sound, colour and smell. What a surprise!

The natural process of dying

I think dying is a very similar process to being born. First, there are the subtle changes in the body signifying that something has changed, which may only be apparent to the person experiencing them. Energy levels may decrease and appetites reduce. The body becomes leaner and eventually wasted as the signs that the body is failing become more apparent. Life becomes wearisome, and the pain and discomfort associated with illness increase. Drugs used to mask the pain cause their own set of physical problems, with constipation, nausea and drowsiness being common. Chemotherapy and radiation are withdrawn as they become less effective and illness becomes more established.

As the person's energy saps away, more and more time is spent in bed or in a chair resting. Life and everyday tasks become difficult. Everything is an effort. As with advanced pregnancy and impending labour, the body prepares for the final process of dying.

There are a number of signs that death is near.

Increased fatigue and weariness

Illness uses up energy. As this energy is depleted, everyday activities become impossible. Eventually, even getting up out of bed is exhausting and no longer possible. Assistance is required with all activities and even the simple act of swallowing may become difficult.

Lack of interest in one's surroundings

The excitement of life is lost, and hobbies or activities once enjoyed are no longer appealing. Watching football on television or reading a favourite novel is not worth the effort. Assets worth millions of dollars are no longer important. Everyday things that used to be important no longer have value. Visitors are a burden. Most of the time is spent asleep or resting. Sleep is a friend.

Loss of appetite

Eating is too much effort, and the thought of food may even be distressing. That favourite apple pie loses its appeal. Cigarettes are not needed and alcohol unwanted.

Increased confusion and restlessness

Like wearing a pair of ill-fitting shoes or wearing a scratchy woollen garment, it is as if the body no longer fits. The result is restlessness and fidgeting as the "discomfort of illness" increases. In addition, the brain, subject as it is to the chemical changes associated with dying, becomes confused. Restlessness, agitation and hallucinations are common, and consciousness gradually decreases.

Abnormal breathing

Breathing becomes irregular as death approaches. Deep breaths are followed by shorter episodes of breathing, and there are times – long times – when no breathing occurs.

The breathing also becomes noisy and rattly as secretions in the back of the throat gurgle away. This abnormal breathing does not cause the person distress, but it can be quite distressing to witness.

Unexplained dramatic improvement in health

For unknown reasons, some people who are obviously dying paradoxically dramatically improve in health a few days or hours before they die. They go from a state of impending death to being the life of the party. They sit up and chat and feel well enough to eat. Their energy levels increase, and it seems as if the prospect of dying has been a false alarm. This unexplained episode of revitalisation is bonus time to enjoy with family and friends.

The time of dying

These signs are not absolute or definitive but should rather be viewed as a signal that death is near. As with labour, dying cannot be rushed or avoided. Some people may take days to die, others require hours. And, as with labour, death is something for which the body is prepared.

ASSETS WORTH MILLIONS OF DOLLARS ARE NO LONGER IMPORTANT. EVERYDAY THINGS THAT USED TO BE IMPORTANT NO LONGER HAVE VALUE.

There is no denying that the time of dying is a period of distress and suffering. The body struggles with the limitations placed on it as life draws to an end. Pain is often part of the dying process and the thing many people fear the most. The role of the palliative care team cannot be overemphasised during this turbulent time. These people are the "saints of medicine", providing compassionate medical care to minimise the pain and other symptoms associated with dying. Just as midwives and obstetricians assist during the difficult time of labour, so these professionals provide valuable assistance during the difficult time of dying.

There seems to be a compensatory mechanism whereby the distress associated with dying is diminished at the very end as life is passing away. It begins with emotional and social withdrawal before death and leads up to decreased consciousness during the final hours. Dying people are not aware of their bowel

FOR UNKNOWN REASONS, SOME PEOPLE WHO ARE OBVIOUSLY DYING PARADOXICALLY DRAMATICALLY IMPROVE IN HEALTH A FEW DAYS OR HOURS BEFORE THEY DIE.

functions or thirst or need for air. The whole event is often a blur – a foggy, confused process. Some people leave this mortal life in peace; others with a struggle.

At some point the flame of life flickers and then no longer burns. Somewhere in the battle between life and death, it becomes quiet and peaceful. The body is at rest.

As with the travails of birth, dying is also a storm. It rages for a while and then passes by. What was our greatest fear is to be feared no more. Death brings an end to a life, but not necessarily a life to an end.

Death is impersonal. It has no favourites and regards all of us as equal. Although death is a biological process and a natural part of everyday life, we cannot help feeling the enormous pain and loss associated with dying. We suffer the consequences of having emotion. We are human after all.

THE EMOTIONS OF DYING ARE IMPORTANT AND ALL TOO OFTEN THEY ARE NEGLECTED BECAUSE THEY ARE SO PERSONAL.

Dying is not only a physical event it is also a profound emotional experience. A skilled physician can readily manage the physical symptoms associated with dying. Managing the emotional aspects of dying is a far more challenging. The emotions of dying are important and all too often they are neglected because they are so personal. Each person deserves honesty when it comes to emotions.

Chapter 5: The Emotions of Dying

If your time ain't come,
not even a doctor can kill you.
– American proverb

There is no mercy or pity in nature. A lion does not feel remorse at hunting down the young and weak antelope calf. Equally, the young doe moves on, leaving the lifeless carcass of her offspring to the lion. No bitter tears are shed. After the excitement of the hunt, the nervous antelope herd returns to the business of grazing. There is only an increased sense of wariness and a restlessness that soon passes. In nature, death is not a tragedy but an everyday part of life. Life goes on as the herd moves on.

We have very powerful emotions, emotions that strongly influence and determine our complex behaviour. They are generated in response to stimuli and based on our previous experiences and behaviours. From our earliest years, our emotions drive our behaviour; the temper tantrums of the terrible twos are perhaps the expression of emotion in its purest (but not necessarily most constructive) form. Our behaviour and emotions are intertwined.

Emotions, when mixed with imagination, can get the better of us if we allow them to. While expressing emotion is a good thing, irrational and uncontrolled emotion can be destructive. Understanding our emotions enables us to better understand, accept and, if necessary, control our behaviour.

> OUR BEHAVIOUR AND EMOTIONS ARE INTERTWINED. EMOTIONS, WHEN MIXED WITH IMAGINATION, CAN GET THE BETTER OF US IF WE ALLOW THEM TO.

Emotions are powerful

We all experience powerful emotions at times. These can range from the exhilaration and ecstasy of winning to the debilitating depression or explosive anger of losing.

Emotions are irrational

We are blessed, or perhaps cursed, with an extraordinary range of emotions. We feel guilt, anger, love, empathy, hate, joy and sorrow, to name but a few. Our emotions cause us to behave irrationally and illogically. Think of the irrational behaviour we all often exhibit as teenagers first falling in love. Emotions such as compassion, empathy and fear enable people to perform tasks of great courage and heroism, sometimes saving others at the cost of their own lives. Equally, emotions of hatred, anger or fear have motivated thousands to go to war and kill others. It is our emotions that make us so human.

Emotions make us vulnerable

Sometimes our emotions can so overpower us that they dramatically influence our behaviour. Being emotionally overwhelmed can be a source of terrible shame and embarrassment, particularly in our modern society in which exhibiting powerful emotion is frequently frowned upon. We have learnt that revealing our feelings is a sign of weakness and that we ought to behave with appropriate decorum in the face of emotional distress. Boys don't cry, do they?

EMOTIONS SUCH AS COMPASSION, EMPATHY AND FEAR ENABLE PEOPLE TO PERFORM TASKS OF GREAT COURAGE AND HEROISM

Crying, however, is a natural response to emotional distress, as laughter is to an enjoyable emotional experience. We cry and laugh much less in the world of today. We try so hard to control our emotions, but it is truly our emotions that control us.

Emotions need to be expressed

Bottling up emotions is as futile as trying to prevent water flowing from a spring. If you block the flow of water in one direction, it flows in another direction. If it is plugged, it builds up sufficient pressure to break out in some other way. Even if the flow is supressed, the water remains ready to be released at some future date. Like water, emotions need to flow. They need to be released. Supressed emotion results in both physical and emotional harm.

Emotions persist

If you have been to see a good movie, such as one where the hero wins the girl and saves the world, chances are you will come away feeling good and pumped up. These feelings may last for a few minutes to a few hours before fading away. More dramatic events, such as graduating or winning a prize, may leave you feeling euphoric for days.

Some emotions, however, don't disappear completely. They become entrenched and persist. Often the emotions that linger are negative emotions related to a past injury or insult, which are easily triggered by later events. These emotions may become so dysfunctional that they affect be-

BEING AWARE OF OUR EMOTIONS IS IMPORTANT BECAUSE IT GIVES US THE OPPORTUNITY TO RETAIN CONTROL WHEN THE RIDE SEEMS TO BE OUT OF CONTROL.

haviour throughout life. Dealing with past emotions is often challenging.

Emotions are affected by circumstance

It is natural to react with emotion to life's circumstances. Very few people remain emotionally detached from life events. Consider your emotional response to the following set of circumstances:

- Being late for a meeting and stuck in gridlock traffic.
- Winning the national lottery.
- Finding your lost wallet.
- Getting lost in a city.
- Meeting a dear old friend.
- Meeting an old enemy from school.

Life is a rollercoaster ride of emotion, ranging from happy highs to depressive lows and back up again. Most of us live our lives with the expectation that the ride will be mostly fun, or at least one for which we won't demand our money back at the end. Sometimes, however, the ride is going to be traumatic whether we like it or not.

Being aware of our emotions is important because it gives us the opportunity to retain control when the ride seems to be out of control. Because emotion affects behaviour, uncontrolled emotion can be harmful or even dangerous. Many relationships suffer irreversible damage in a storm of uncontrolled emotion.

Expressing emotions is difficult, particularly when the emotions are painful and associated with loss. As much as talking about emotions can be difficult, not talking about them is worse. No one can guess how you are feeling. Often we are not fully conscious of our own emotions let alone anyone else's. Dealing with deep emotional issues is not easy.

ALTHOUGH EACH PERSON HAS AN INDIVIDUAL SET OF EMOTIONS, UNIQUE EMOTIONAL TRIGGERS AND THEIR OWN WAYS OF DEALING WITH EMOTIONS, IN DYING THERE ARE COMMON EMOTIONS THAT WE ALL FEEL.

Talking about the emotions relating to death and dying is *so difficult* that very few people ever do fully address how they are feeling. Sometimes these emotions are buried so deeply that no one realises the emotions were ever there. These emotions are painful. They are powerful. They are irrational. They make us vulnerable. They persist. They change with circumstances. But they are also natural.

There are many emotional responses associated with dying. Although each person has an individual set of emotions, unique emotional triggers and their own ways of dealing with emotions, in dying there are common emotions that we all feel.

Chapter 6: The Emotion of Fear

Fear is only as deep as the mind allows
– Japanese proverb

Think back to the last time you were afraid. Do you remember the effect it had on you? Perhaps you can recall your heart pounding in your chest, your breath coming in shallow gasps and the sweat pouring from you. Events may have appeared to happen automatically and in slow motion. These responses to the emotion of fear are perfectly natural.

Fear is an essential emotion. On a basic evolutionary level, it is a behavioural response to an actual or perceived threat. Fear is a protective mechanism; its purpose is to ensure survival. When we are frightened, our bodies release the hormone adrenalin. Adrenalin arms us for fight or flight. It allows us to perform extraordinary feats to escape danger or protect loved ones. Take, for example, a recent news report about a young lady who lifted a motor vehicle off her father when he became trapped under the car in a freak accident. Fear can be a good thing.

The bigger, uglier brother of fear is anxiety. Whereas fear is an acceptable response to a direct (or perceived) threat, anxiety is a powerful emotional response to an imagined threat. Anxiety may be so powerful that it changes behaviour for the worse and becomes debilitating. Managing anxiety is difficult because it is irrational and anxious fears can be lodged deep in the imagination, where there are no limits and anything is possible. Our anxieties can become our worst nightmares.

> MANAGING ANXIETY
> IS DIFFICULT BECAUSE
> IT IS IRRATIONAL AND
> ANXIOUS FEARS CAN BE
> LODGED DEEP IN
> THE IMAGINATION.

Consider, for a minute, the great white shark. This is a magnificent creature, minding its own business as it effortlessly glides through the ocean. Yet the great white is capable of hunting and tearing its prey to shreds with its razor sharp teeth in a matter of seconds. Great whites are the dominant predators within their oceanic domain.

If I were to find myself in the ocean surrounded by these creatures, I would have every reason to be afraid. My fear would prompt me to take definitive action to get out of the danger zone. Once safe (it is to be hoped) on board a boat, I would experience the after effects of extreme fear. I would be shaking as my muscles tried to manage the surge of adrenalin. My heart would be pounding in my chest and I would be breathing rapidly. I might feel nauseous and even vomit. It would not be unusual to experience an uncontrolled release of emotion such as sobbing or crying. Eventually I would begin to breathe normally as my fear diminished and the threat to my life passed.

BEING AFRAID OF DEATH IS A NATURAL RESPONSE TO DANGER. OUR FEAR PROTECTS US AND PREVENTS US FROM DOING ANYTHING THAT WILL POTENTIALLY RESULT IN DEATH.

If I were sitting at home safe on dry land, my fear of great white sharks would be laughable. These creatures with their sharp teeth and cunning black eyes would be no threat at all. But if I had *galeophobia*, the fear of sharks, I would continue to be terrified of sharks even though there would be no possibility of a shark attacking me on land. People with *galeophobia* may even fear the possibility of a shark attack when taking a shower! I struggled with *galeophobia* after the movie *Jaws* was released, imagining the possibility of great whites appearing in the swimming pool. As ridiculous as it seems now, my anxiety was real enough to modify my behaviour and cause distress.

Anxiety can take many forms: phobias of spiders, of open spaces or closed spaces, or even a fear of public speaking, are all examples of anxiety. Phobias are extreme expressions of anxiety, but we all experience some form of anxiety at times. This is because we are intelligent, thinking creatures. We can imagine outcomes, and if combined with negative past experiences and subconscious processes, we may be in for a rough time.

Being afraid of death is a natural response to danger. Our fear protects us and prevents us from doing anything that will potentially result in death. We know that we won't be able to avoid death forever. As we have seen, the events around dying seem to take care of themselves. The challenge is managing the anxiety related to death and dying.

Initially, anxiety is based on some degree of reality. It is normal to be concerned about future events and how they may affect us. People facing death have many concerns. For example:

Will I be at home or in a hospital?
Will I drop dead in the shopping centre?
Will I be alone?
Will my wife and kids be okay?
What will happen to my pets?
Who will sell my house?
What will become of my garden?
What if I am not dead and they bury me alive?
Will my wife run off with another man?
Will this be the end of my existence?
Can I expect a judgement and punishment?

These questions, and many like them, are quite normal and rational. They require our attention. They allow us to plan and prepare for if and when these events occur. The trouble is that our normal anxieties can quickly blaze out of control. Fired on by our wild imagination, the anxiety of death may become quite extreme. If left unchecked, our anxiety can result in severe distress and dysfunction.

Whoa! A touch of reality may be needed.

Is the threat real or is it imagined?

If the threat is imagined, then the outcome of what is being imagined can be changed. Instead of focusing on a disastrous outcome, change your thinking and imagine a different ending. I know this is a gross oversimplification of anxiety and fear, but try it. Change the ending of the story to be a good one.

Because our anxieties are based on our previous life experiences, we may sometimes find it impossible to consider a better outcome. However, reality often doesn't turn out as we imagined it. Yes, life is full of unpleasant little surprises, and I am sure that we all have stories about times in our life that have gone horribly wrong. I bet that when things turned out disastrously, however, events somehow took care of

THE EVENTS AROUND DYING SEEM TO TAKE CARE OF THEMSELVES. THE CHALLENGE IS MANAGING THE ANXIETY RELATED TO DEATH AND DYING.

themselves. Like being caught in a gigantic wave, we are frequently swept uncontrollably along with no real opportunity to change events as they unfolded. Being anxious did little to change the outcome, and anxiety no doubt made things worse, if anything.

Being apprehensive about dying is perfectly normal. We fear what we don't know. I believe that no one goes to his or her death without being affected by fear in some way. Each person is different, and the fear and anxiety that each of us experience will be founded in a unique, personal story. There is nothing wrong with this normal emotional response. But fear can get out of control if it is allowed to.

EXPOSING OUR FEARS AND EMOTIONS MAKES US STRONGER AND NOT WEAKER. SHARE YOUR FEELINGS WITH SOMEONE YOU TRUST AND ALLOW THEM TO HELP CARRY YOUR BURDEN.

Life is too short to be tormented and trapped in a cage of imagined fears.

Anxiety of death can be very severe, and professional assistance may be required to untangle and manage our fears if they are unbearable. Exposing our fears and emotions makes us stronger and not weaker. Share your feelings with someone you trust and allow them to help carry your burden.

Chapter 7: The Emotion of Loss

Loss and possession, death and life are one,
There falls no shadow where
there shines no sun.
– Hilaire Belloc

L osing is never fun. Missing out or being eliminated from the competition is always unpleasant. We have all dealt with disappointment in life. We may have lost at tennis, missed out on that perfect job, or our loss may have been something as trivial as being the first to be eliminated from a friendly game of cards. The emotions relating to loss are very real and can be very intense. How many shattered tennis rackets have been at the receiving end of a lost point?

Although we may have faced many losses in life, our greatest loss and disappointment comes with the realisation that we are mortal and that our lives are finite. In the game of life we all eventually lose and we will all eventually be eliminated from the game. There are no winners, only those left behind to continue without us.

It takes time to work through the disappointment associated with loss. In her book, *On Death and Dying* (1969), Dame Elisabeth Kübler-Ross described five stages of loss associated with dying. These stages of emotion are often blurred, they don't necessarily all occur and people do not necessarily move through each stage in order.

Understanding these powerful emotions allows things to be put into perspective. Moving through the emotions takes time and it cannot be rushed or forced. The end result is hopefully acceptance, but it need not be. Being aware of the stage you are at may make sense of what seems to be a senseless situation.

UNDERSTANDING POWERFUL EMOTIONS ALLOWS THINGS TO BE PUT INTO PERSPECTIVE. MOVING THROUGH THE EMOTIONS TAKES TIME AND IT CANNOT BE RUSHED OR FORCED.

See if you can recognise the following emotions that Kübler-Ross identifies as being associated with dying.

1. Denial

Consider what your reaction might be to the news that a category five hurricane was fast approaching. Your first emotion might be denial. This is a powerful ally when we are given bad news. Denial is perfectly normal for a while. It buys us time to think and reflect and process the grim news. Denial may be a quite obvious reaction when the news is first broken to you.

There will never be a storm! It won't happen!

Denial can also be insidious, allowing us to accept the bad news and then pretend that the terrible event isn't happening. It is like turning our back to the storm. People in denial fail to feel the strong wind and see the flashes of lightning. They refuse to hear the booming thunder, explaining it all away as an unrelated event as they happily face the opposite direction. They may continue with business as usual, only accepting the evidence of the raging storm when they are swept away by the howling wind and driving rain. Even in these extreme conditions, some people will refuse to budge from their belief that *everything is just fine!*

EVEN IN EXTREME CONDITIONS, SOME PEOPLE WILL REFUSE TO BUDGE FROM THEIR BELIEF THAT EVERYTHING IS JUST FINE!

When denial continues and becomes entrenched, it prevents people from responding to an event with appropriate behaviour, much to the frustration of friends and family who recognise the severity of the situation and want to respond or move on to action.

2. Anger

Anger is a wonderful emotion. It is powerful and helps people rid themselves of emotional pressure, much like a volcano exploding. The problem is that other people may get injured in the process. Smashing tennis racquets at Wimbledon is one thing, but smashing people is something quite different. We feel angry when we don't get our way, or when things are outside of our control and we face a loss. Standing in endless queues, being trapped in gridlock traffic or being ignored are things that make me angry because I have no control of the situation.

ANGER MAY NOT ALWAYS BE EXPLOSIVE. SOMETIMES ANGER IS EXPRESSED PASSIVELY WITH AVOIDANCE, MANIPULATION, OBSESSIVE BEHAVIOUR OR BEING OVERLY CRITICAL.

Anger may not always be explosive. Sometimes anger is expressed passively with avoidance, manipulation, obsessive behaviour or being overly critical. There is always someone at the receiving end of anger. There is always someone else or something to blame.

If we consider our category 5 Hurricane again, angry responses might be:

> *What have I done to deserve this?*
> *It's your fault for bringing us here on holiday*
> *in the first place!*
> *You always bring bad luck; you are an ill omen.*

In the face of incurable disease such as cancer, the comments may be even more destructive.

> *It's fine for you to be cheerful and happy, but*
> *you're not the one dying.*
> *You will probably find a new husband as soon*
> *as I'm gone and spend all my money.*
> *You don't care about me and you can't wait for*
> *me to die.*

Those in the firing line have a tough time as this phase of emotion rages on.

It is important to recognise and discuss anger and its effects. This may save relationships and friendships during difficult times. Anger is a natural emotion to feel, but it does little to change circumstances.

In facing the prospect of our own death, we need to keep in mind that those who love and care for us may never have been in this situation before. They are not sure how to react. They may also be angry and going through the same process of loss.

3. Bargaining
Who can resist a good bargain?

As anger and denial fail to change our circumstances, a new strategy emerges: bargaining. As the reality of dying sets in, the process of buying more time becomes all-important.

> *If I can't live forever, I want to live as long as possible.*

Statements beginning with "perhaps" and "if" are characteristic of this bargaining process. Any price is a bargain if life can be extended. It's during this emotion phase that the charlatans of cancer quackery make their ill-gotten gains. They promise miraculous cures, exploiting people who find themselves in this vulnerable position. They promise extra time in the rapidly ending game.

> *If I drink this juice, then perhaps I might get better.*
> *I will try this treatment because it may allow me another two months of survival.*
> *I know of a doctor who has these drops that cured someone else.*

Bargaining may be more subtle.

> *I will do well and live a good life because perhaps God will then let me live longer.*
> *I will bake those cookies for the bowling club*

and help Tom build his shed because perhaps
these good deeds will count for me living longer.

The process of bargaining continues through to the next phase of emotion. Reality sets in and the obvious becomes apparent. Life will end. It cannot continue forever.

4. Depression

The next emotion is depression.

The game is lost and there is a realisation that life is ending. The response is grief in the face of this enormous loss. It is time to mourn the loss of our life and things to be left behind: partners, children, family and friends, homes and hard-earned gains.

Sadness and depression are a natural response to this realised loss.

It is hard to find comfort during this time. Time is needed to express and work through the sorrow associated with this loss. Depression may be recognised as an emotion of feeling sad and sorrowful. It may manifest itself by a lack of interest in life's activities, poor appetite and interrupted sleep. There are no pleasures during the episode of depression. It is a black and gloomy period, but it need not last forever.

If the journey is allowed to continue, the period of mourning comes to an end. There is a gradual acceptance of the loss.

5. Acceptance

Acceptance is the final emotion. It is a place of peace and contentment.

I cannot change my circumstances, so I make the best of what I have.

It's here that life can, in a way, start again. There is now an opportunity to make every minute count. What will be, will be. The focus shifts from death and dying to life and living. Death is no longer an enemy but a future event. Life is precious and not to be wasted.

> THERE IS NOW AN OPPORTUNITY TO MAKE EVERY MINUTE COUNT. WHAT WILL BE, WILL BE. THE FOCUS SHIFTS FROM DEATH AND DYING TO LIFE AND LIVING. DEATH IS NO LONGER AN ENEMY BUT A FUTURE EVENT.

The life that remains becomes a celebration. Pleasure is found in simple things, such as feeling the warmth of the sun, hearing the sweet sound of birds or seeing the great Southern Cross in the vast evening sky. It's a time to reflect on life and remember the good things. It is a time to live life to the very last precious drop.

Each emotion is unique. Not everyone experiences all of these emotions. Some people manage loss with humour, others with heightened activity. Working through the emotions of loss is a journey that takes time. It starts with bad news, it requires a period of adjustment and, hopefully, it ends with an acceptance that this is all a normal part of life.

The period of adjustment is variable from person to person. It may be easier for some and very distressing to others. Loss is a two-way street affecting those who face dying as well as those who are witness to the process. Talking about these feelings and recognising the process of loss may make the journey easier. Seek professional help if your emotions or those of others close to you are so severe and dysfunctional that they cause injury and ongoing distress.

Chapter 8: Guilt and Emotional Pain

"It spills itself in fearing to be spilt."
– William Shakespeare, *Hamlet*

Take a moment to think back to when you did something wrong as a youngster. Perhaps you stole the apples off your neighbour's tree, or secretly smoked a prohibited cigarette at school. Regardless of whether you were caught out or not, the chances are that your behaviour changed, if only for a short while. You may have avoided the neighbour for a time, or reacted differently to your parents. This changed behaviour was driven by the emotion of guilt.

Guilt can be described as the feeling of responsibility for having committed an offence. We feel guilty when we do something wrong. Often, we have no more than a perception of having committed a bad act. Guilt is inextricably linked to our conscience, which is how we differentiate between what we think is right and wrong.

We may rationalise our guilt, laughing off our "fruit-stealing venture" as no more than a childish prank. We may blame the victim, citing their selfishness in not picking the apples themselves and leaving them to rot on the ground. We may justify our behaviour on the basis that we were hungry.

> GUILT IS INEXTRICABLY LINKED TO OUR CONSCIENCE, WHICH IS HOW WE DIFFERENTIATE BETWEEN WHAT WE THINK IS RIGHT AND WRONG.

Regardless of our excuses, we have a compelling need to rid ourselves of guilt. Unresolved guilt leads to shame, and these are powerful and damaging emotions.

There are at least three types of guilt associated with advanced illness.

The guilt of survivorship

Those who survive while others die suffer guilt. They may feel it is wrong or unfair to live while the ones they love have to die. They feel guilty that life remains theirs to enjoy. They feel guilty about their health and their vitality, and ashamed of occasionally having unkind thoughts about those who are struggling with advanced illness.

> *I wish it was all over.*
> *I wish that he would die; I can't bear to see him*
> *suffering like this.*

This guilt may result in changed behaviour, which does not go unnoticed and results in further guilt. The spiral of emotion and behaviour can, if permitted to do so, spin out of control quite easily.

In the whirlpool of emotion some thoughts will be wrong, unkind or unreasonable. These thoughts, however, are perfectly natural and no more than a normal response to the distress of chronic illness. Accepting these thoughts and feelings as normal and not something to be ashamed of is an important step in minimising survivorship guilt.

The guilt of dying

Life is precious, and in society we do all that we can to save lives. Vast amounts of money are spent on saving lives. Medical shows on television emphasise the importance of saving a life and a death is consid-

THE SPIRAL OF EMOTION AND BEHAVIOUR CAN, IF PERMITTED TO DO SO, SPIN OUT OF CONTROL QUITE EASILY.

ered a failure. In our western society dying is strictly forbidden. A dying person is guilty of a number of serious offences:

> Dying is **expensive**; there are already so many
> costs and now there's the extra financial
> burden of the funeral and flowers and so on.
> Dying is **inconsiderate**; it is going to upset the
> niece's wedding plans.
> Dying is **selfish**; who is going to mow the lawn
> or clean the house if I am not there?
> Dying is **rebellious**; everyone expects me to get
> better.

Dying must rate as the ultimate wrong. If ever you want to upset someone's day, go ahead and die. Yet how can we be held responsible for something so completely out of our control?

Feeling guilt and shame about dying may cause tremendous distress. In most cases, however, blame for the fact that you are dying cannot be attributed to anyone. Ask yourself, "Is it something I've done on purpose; do I have anything to do with the fact that I'm now dying?" If not, let go of the guilt; it has no place. If you *have*

IF YOU HAVE DONE SOMETHING TO AFFECT YOUR SURVIVAL, IT IS TIME TO FORGIVE YOURSELF AND MOVE ON.

done something to affect your survival, it is time to forgive yourself and move on. No one is perfect.

The guilt of the past

We sometimes do silly things we regret later in life. The wrongs we have done cannot always be undone, and we live with the guilt of our offence. For some, it may have been a trivial matter, easily forgiven. For others, the guilt of the offence remains a severe burden throughout life. As death approaches, this guilt can become unbearable as there seems to be no way to make amends and no apparent way forward.

Guilt results in a compensatory change in behaviour. Some examples of changed behaviour include:

- Overcompensation: to do, be, and get everything right.
- Oversensitivity at doing anything wrong.
- Withdrawal: hiding away from any responsibility.
- Denial: rationalising and pretending nothing's wrong.
- Punishment: inflicting lifetime punishment (often on ourselves) for doing something wrong.

This guilt is easily removed by forgiveness, but forgiveness is not always available. The magnitude of the offence may be (or may seem to be) too severe to expect forgiveness. The offended person may no longer be in a position to offer forgiveness. Even when it is offered, it may not be possible for the person to accept that he or she has been forgiven. The guilt may still linger. Ultimate forgiveness is from God but that requires faith and faith comes later.

Guilt and pain

Guilt may cause pain. We use words like torture, agony and torment to describe the cruelty of pain. Pain is not always physical. We may also feel emotional pain – feelings that cause us immense distress and suffering.

Emotional pain is often more chronic and severe than physical pain. Physical pain is easily controlled with morphine, or even anaesthetic if need be, but what controls emotional pain? Powerful negative and painful emotions cannot be eliminated, and often they are numbed by substance abuse. Vast quantities of alcohol or drugs may dull the pain, but it may never go away unless we permit ourselves to let the pain go.

ULTIMATE FORGIVENESS IS FROM GOD BUT THAT REQUIRES FAITH AND FAITH COMES LATER.

The severity of emotional pain that a person can feel is illustrated in the story told by Baroness Finlay of Llandaff, a professor of palliative medicine at the Cardiff University School of Medicine. Baroness Finlay was attending to a woman who had terminal cancer and who was in severe pain. As much as the palliative carers tried, they were unable to settle the unbearable pain the woman was experiencing, and she continued to cry out in terrible anguish. There was no apparent medical explanation for the pain, and no medication to settle it.

IS IT WRONG TO DIE?

NO.

Baroness Finlay struggled with the dilemma of the woman's unresolved pain. After attending an important dinner and still dressed in her formal evening gown, she returned to the ward to find the woman in distress. Baroness Finlay sat next to the patient and allowed her to talk, taking time to hear her story. She realised that the woman was suffering unbearable emotional pain at the thought of having to die and leave her young children. Once the cause of the pain was established, a program of care was started. The massive doses of morphine were reduced as the patient was allowed to work through the emotions associated with dying.

There are many reasons to suffer emotional pain when facing death. The guilt of dying should not be one of them. Many people face death with the recognition there is nothing they can do about it. They may in fact look forward to their release from illness and physical suffering.

IT IS ACCEPTABLE

TO DIE.

Nonetheless, many people feel guilt about dying, and I believe that too many people suffer this terrible guilt.

Is it wrong to die?

NO.

It may be unfair, unwanted or unavoidable, but it is not wrong. It is a natural everyday event beyond our control. The act of dying requires no forgiveness. Asking loved ones for permission to die allows them to be gracious and kind, and accepting of what is natural and normal. It removes the guilt and allows for a time of greater companionship as life fades away.

It is acceptable to die.

Chapter 9: The Emotion of Hope

When the world says, "Give up,"
Hope whispers, "Try it one more time."
– Author unknown

On that fated night of 14 April 1912 when the *Titanic* hit the iceberg, there were three groups of people caught up in the terrible events. The first group comprised of the fortunate ones who had access to the lifeboats and, with this, a possibility of rescue. There was the second group who had no hope of being rescued and who perished on the boat as it sank into the frozen depths of the northern Atlantic Ocean. And then there was the third group, those who ended up in the icy waters clutching desperately to flotsam *in the hope* of being rescued.

What is this strange emotion of hope?

Hope may be defined as the feeling that things will turn out for the best. It is being filled with the possibility that things will improve. It is a powerful emotion that allows us to survive in the most extreme circumstances. Consider the examples of prisoners-of-war in concentration camps, desperate miners trapped underground under kilometres of rock, or shipwrecked mariners drifting on an endless ocean. The reality of their immediate day-to-day circumstances is that nothing will change and their chances of survival are small. Yet they continue hanging on to life in the hope of freedom or rescue.

> HOPE OFFERS US A DIFFERENT PERSPECTIVE. IT IS A PERSPECTIVE THAT REFUSES TO ACCEPT THE OBVIOUS.

Hope offers us a different perspective. It is a perspective that refuses to accept the obvious, that considers alternatives when there seem to be none. Hope is not a certainty that things will get better. It is not a magical "close your eyes and make a wish, and it will all be well" response to hardship. It is not based on fantasy or imagination. Hope is based on the truth and a fundamental recognition of the severity and harsh reality of a situation. Hope is a powerful call-to-action and demands courage.

Without hope we give up; with hope we get up. Having hope does not make the path any easier, but it gives us the impetus to do what it takes to allow for things to possibly get better.

In his book *Good to Great* (2001), Jim Collins tells the compelling story of Admiral Jim Stockdale. This amazing man and war hero was able to survive the terrors of being a captive in the "Hanoi Hilton" prisoner-of-war camp during the Vietnam War. He was tortured twenty-four times in the eight years he was imprisoned.

Stockdale's survival was based on taking the action required to stay alive and his fundamental belief that things would eventually get better. His hope was grounded in dealing with the immediate reality of the situation and his faith that he would eventually be freed. In his account, Stockdale maintained that optimism was the enemy of hope. Optimism is only a wish for action and a better outcome whereas hope demands that we take action towards a better outcome.

IT SEEMS THAT HOPE WILL EVENTUALLY FAIL US AND THAT DEATH WILL HAVE THE FINAL WORD.

Consider the dramatic story of Aron Ralston who amputated his right arm to survive after becoming trapped while canyoneering alone in the Canyonlands National Park, Utah. His story is portrayed in the movie *127 hours*. With his arm trapped under a massive boulder, Ralston knew there was no chance of escape. He wrote his farewell note to his loved ones and prepared to die until he realised that there was another way.

From the absolute evidence that escape was impossible while his arm remained trapped, Ralston came to the realisation that he might escape without his arm. Using blunt tools, he managed to break his arm, and with a dull penknife, he hacked through his flesh to free himself from certain death. Weakened, dehydrated and injured, Ralston then had to find his way back to civilisation. Ralston survived because he dared to look at the ridiculous alternatives. He survived because he considered the impossible possibilities. He survived because he hoped to live.

> HOPE IS A STRONG ALLY IN THE FACE OF HARDSHIP. IT IS NOT A GUARANTEE THAT THINGS WILL TURN OUT FOR THE BETTER, BUT RATHER ACTS AS A COMPASS POINTING US IN THE DIRECTION OF POSSIBILITY.

Hope is a strong ally in the face of hardship. It is not a guarantee that things will turn out for the better, but rather acts as a compass pointing us in the direction of possibility. In illness there may be a hope for cure or a miracle, but there are no guarantees. It seems that hope will eventually fail us and that death will have the final word.

Hope in dying

Is there any hope in dying?

That depends on our perspective and on our willingness to look at the impossible possibilities.

DEATH IS NOT THE END, BUT A TRANSITION INTO ANOTHER DIMENSION. THE PROCESS OF DYING IS LIKE A BUTTERFLY EMERGING FROM A DEAD COCOON.

If death is the end of all things, the final black-out, we are as those perishing aboard the sinking *Titanic*. There is no call-to-action because the situation is hopeless. We begrudgingly have to accept our cruel fate. But if death is not the end of the road, but merely a transition into another dimension, a range of exciting possibilities becomes available. We potentially have more hope than those who waited for rescue as they clung to the flotsam in the dark waters of the Atlantic. We have an opportunity to be as those in the lifeboats, assured of rescue when the crisis has passed.

If death is a doorway, where could it possibly lead?

There is compelling evidence to suggest that there is an existence after death. Death is not the end, but a transition into another dimension. The process of dying is like a butterfly emerging from a dead cocoon.

Dare we have hope in dying?

Chapter 10:
Emotional Responsibility

One thing you can't hide -
is when you're crippled inside.
– John Lennon

How good are you at DIY? Do-it-Yourself can be a curse, and I have discovered that I am terrible at being my own handyman. I blame my parents. My father is the only person I know who was able to set a lawnmower alight in a fiery blaze after carrying out minor repairs.

DIY looks easy and often promises to be the cheaper solution. Invariably, however, the instructions are unreadable, a handful of nuts and bolts are always left over after the project is finished, and the end result never quite looks like the picture on the box cover. I quickly learnt that to get it right usually requires a professional touch.

The same can be said about emotional DIY. Working with emotions may seem easy enough, but invariably it is a difficult task. Emotions that are poorly managed may cause continual offence and hurt to yourself and others. Emotional responsibility is about recognising when emotions are out of control and then doing something about it. It is important to know when emotional DIY is not working.

> WORKING WITH EMOTIONS MAY SEEM EASY ENOUGH, BUT INVARIABLY IT IS A DIFFICULT TASK.

We all experience intense emotions at times. We all have the ability to blow our top and say dumb things, or act foolishly or defensively when threatened. Ridding ourselves of emotion and blowing off steam is normal and healthy provided no one else is habitually injured in the process. There is a big difference between what may be an everyday skirmish and a full-on war.

Facing a serious illness or death makes us increasingly vulnerable to threat or injury. Our emotions are felt more intensely as our coping skills are worn thin by chronic emotional bombardment. It is easy to be caught up in a whirlwind of emotion, and this emotion can be downright dangerous. What starts off as a small insignificant thing can soon spiral out of control. Emotional responsibility is about managing emotions before they become an emotional tornado weaving a path of destruction in people's lives. It takes real courage to develop a disaster management plan for out-of-control emotions.

Optimism is not a good disaster management plan. Life is not always fair or kind. Sugar-coated goodness is not one of life's realities. Life can be tough, and hardship happens; coping with this hardship is a necessary life skill.

Another ineffective strategy is to ignore or deny oneself from experiencing emotions. Intense emotions will inevitably be felt in circumstances in which someone is expecting to die. These powerful emotions will be felt by all involved: those facing the loss and those sharing the loss. If the thought of dying causes no emotional distress, then either the facts or the reality of the situation have not been fully understood. Dying is associated with real emotions that need to be managed.

EMOTIONAL RESPONSIBILITY IS ABOUT MANAGING EMOTIONS BEFORE THEY BECOME AN EMOTIONAL TORNADO.

An emotional disaster management plan should encompass the following tactics:

Recognise that emotions come and go

Emotions change. Our feelings, whether positive or negative, do not remain the same forever. Sometimes just hanging in there is all we need to do. Taking time out to find shelter until the emotional storm has passed is sometimes a useful tactic. Often, what seems unbearable today may become bearable tomorrow.

Acknowledge emotions and their impact on behaviour

Our behaviour is affected by our emotions. If the behaviour of a loved one has changed, this may be due to their struggle with a range of emotions. People may seem to withdraw as they come to terms with their emotions; it does not mean they don't care.

Express the emotions

Talking about the way we feel is often very difficult, particularly if the emotion is intense and raw and painful. Knowing where to start is often hard. Picking the right time to discuss our emotions can frequently be a challenge.

> DON'T DWELL ON YOUR EMOTIONS AND LET THEM FESTER.

Sometimes emotions can be expressed indirectly. Physical touch is a good way to show you care. Writing about your feelings in a letter allows time to reflect on emotions, and may be an easier way to express emotions without being caught up in the moment.

Sometimes just venting feelings is important. Finding a way to let off steam is essential to good emotional health. Try exercise such as running or boxing. Write your story in prose or poetry. Take up an activity such as painting, meditation, cooking, sewing or reading. Do whatever it takes to calm intense emotions and allow the storm to pass.

Talk about the emotions

No one I know can read minds. It is impossible to know what people are thinking unless they tell you. Sure, they may not be truthful in the telling, but at least it is a starting point.

> DON'T EXPECT OTHERS TO KNOW WHAT YOU ARE FEELING AND DON'T IMAGINE YOU KNOW WHAT OTHERS ARE GOING THROUGH.

Don't expect others to know what you are feeling and don't imagine you know what others are going through. Get the facts by talking. When the emotional storm is under control, talk about the way you feel and ask how other people are feeling.

Accept the emotions and move on

Emotions may be intense, and anger may well up. No one is perfect. When emotions flare up, try to move on as fast as possible. Don't dwell on your emotions and let them fester. Accept that things could have been done better, learn from the experience and move on. We all make mistakes and say unkind things. Use the words "sorry" and "I forgive you" as often as needed because these words often keep the door open to further communication.

Friendships and companionship are built up over years. They require trust and commitment. Don't let an emotional outburst destroy a lifetime of good memories. Maintain your friendships. Friends see each other through the tough times; they hang in there for each other and watch each other's back. Take one on the chin for your friend every now and then.

Recognise when there's a problem

Sadly, there is often a background of suppressed unhappiness in many relationships that comes to a head during a stressful event such as an illness. Years of bitterness can overflow into a flood of unhappiness during times of crisis.

It is also the case that some people are just plain nasty and unpleasant. They suck the life out of others and are abusive and cause harm to the people close to them. They are bullies, and in extreme cases, psychopaths. We have all met people like this. If you are unfortunate enough to be in a close relationship with a person such as this, seek help from elsewhere because it won't be an easy journey in the face of dying.

So many patients of mine have struggled through their final illness alone. They have no close friends and are estranged from their relatives. They have no one willing to assist them in their time of need. Sometimes the reason for this is because they have been a tornado of emotional destruction to others. If you happen to be one of these difficult people, don't despair. Get help.

If our emotional response continually causes personal injury or offence to others, it's a good indicator that an emotional

DIY approach is not working. In life, we sign up for friendliness, kindness, happiness, companionship and fellowship. When emotional distress results in broken relationships, there is a problem. The final product is not looking anything like the picture on the box. It's time to call the professionals!

It's often a good idea to seek professional support when you are emotionally distressed or the cause of distress to other people. Speak to someone you can trust, such as your doctor. Get referred to a psychologist, or speak to a counsellor, psychiatrist, pastor, or even the man on the park bench. Sometimes

SOMETIMES ALL IT TAKES IS ANOTHER PERSPECTIVE. IN THESE CIRCUMSTANCES, DON'T DO EMOTIONAL DIY. IF YOU DO NEED HELP, GET HELP.

all it takes is another perspective. In these circumstances, don't do emotional DIY. If you do need help, get help.

Sometimes more than emotional DIY and professional help are needed. As humans, we are also spiritual entities. There is compelling evidence to suggest that we have a soul, that we exist after death and that the welfare of the soul is important. These spiritual issues also influence emotions and overall wellness. As much as they may seem trivial, they cannot be ignored.

Chapter 11: Introduction to Spirituality

Every man must do two things alone;
he must do his own believing
and his own dying.
– Martin Luther

Have you considered what makes us human?

Biologically, we are animals. The secrets of how our bodies work on a cellular and functional level are derived from the study of animal biology. In some respects, however, we are not very good animals. From an evolutionary perspective, we seem to have done pretty poorly. Compared with our evolutionary cousins the chimpanzees, we have lost the advantage of enormous physical strength.

In comparison with other animals, we have poor vision, an appalling sense of smell and our hearing has devolved to the point of needing hearing aids at the age of fifty.

Socially, we are also disadvantaged. Generally speaking, the behaviour of many animals is instinctive – relative to reproduction, defence and survival of the species. Their needs don't go beyond food and shelter. We, on the other hand, are more difficult to please; we seem to require so much more. What's more, our needs and behaviour sometimes seem to contrast starkly to our biological need to propagate the species. We prey on each other, rob each other of life's resources, diminish our reproductive ability and destroy the ecosystem we are so reliant upon. We covet useless objects such as gold and silver, and desire what others have.

IN CONJUNCTION WITH OUR ABILITY TO EXPRESS OURSELVES THROUGH LANGUAGE, WE HAVE THE LEGACY OF ANCIENT STORIES, MYTHS AND LEGENDS.

On the other hand, we have an irrefutable advantage over other animals. We are exceptionally creative and able to produce exquisite music and beautiful art. We have the ability to communicate our thoughts and feelings through language and laughter. Our attributes, such as compassion, creativity and language, are what make us uniquely human and separate us from other species.

What provides us with this advantage? Is it intellect alone?

I believe that our humanity is defined by our past. In conjunction with our ability to express ourselves through language, we have the legacy of ancient stories, myths and legends. These have been passed down from generation to generation by word of mouth or in sacred writings. The universal message of these stories is that we are more than biological entities. We have spiritual roots.

Many sacred writings, such as those of the Jewish Torah, the Christian Bible, the Islamic Qur'an, the ancient Hindu Texts or the teachings of Buddha, and myths, such as those of Māori, African, Ancient Greek or Ancient Egyptian cultures, are founded on a fundamental belief that the origin and nature of humanity is from the gods.

Our unique spiritual awareness is what differentiates us from other animals. We have an undeniable link to deity. We have a dual nature, being both physical and spiritual creatures. It is this dual nature that makes us profoundly vulnerable to the forces of good and evil. We are governed by a powerful sense of right and wrong, however broad this definition may be. We are driven by greater purposes than reproduction, satisfying hunger and finding shelter. We seek meaning in life and aim for self-actualisation. There is a deeper hunger within us that is never fully satisfied unless we are also spiritually satisfied.

> WE HAVE AN UNDENIABLE LINK TO DEITY. WE HAVE A DUAL NATURE, BEING BOTH PHYSICAL AND SPIRITUAL CREATURES.

However, the problem is that the spiritual realm

is invisible and poorly defined. While we can rely on our physical senses to define this world, they have no use in the spiritual realm. We cannot see, hear, taste, smell or feel spiritual things. They remain hidden, mysterious and elusive. We are seemingly powerless to discover spiritual truths alone but must rely on the revela-

THERE IS EVIDENCE TO SUGGEST AN INVISIBLE SPIRITUAL DIMENSION DOES EXIST.

tions of prophets, teachers and sages. Religion helps us to define and navigate the invisible spiritual dimension, but it is not without its limitations.

Spirituality and spiritual practices are very real to millions of people. Whether they are part of an established religion or a pagan belief, there is evidence to suggest an invisible spiritual dimension does exist.

Is all this spirituality important?

Spirituality *was* important to people in the past. For example, the Ancient Egyptians took extraordinary care to provide for their kings in the afterlife, evidenced by the construction of elaborate pyramids. Spirituality was acceptable across every culture as people looked to the gods for their identity. The major religions of the world affirm the place of spirituality in the history of humanity.

Spirituality is important to the practitioners of modern day faith who live their lives with care in anticipation of reward and accountability in the afterlife. Jews, Christians, Muslims, Hindus, Buddhists and others stop to recognise a god or life-force as they perceive God.

Spirituality *will* be important in the afterlife. If death is a doorway into the spiritual dimension, what lies beyond the door? Our spiritual health and vitality are important considerations. There is more to dying than meets the eye. The sum of our lives is far greater than a handful of ash at the end of a cremation ceremony. Evidence suggests that we are destined for an appointment with God.

> THERE IS MORE TO DYING THAN MEETS THE EYE. THE SUM OF OUR LIVES IS FAR GREATER THAN A HANDFUL OF ASH AT THE END OF A CREMATION CEREMONY.

Exploring spirituality is challenging because it is intangible. It does require a leap of faith, a comment on religion and an open mind. It is not possible to explore spirituality without the risk of treading on a number of delicate toes. It is easier to discuss spirituality if we agree to not absolutely define what is right or wrong.

Exploring the spiritual dimension is not without reward. It is a journey that offers the promise of life after death, eternal happiness, being reunited with loved ones and friendship with God.

Is it too good to be true? Discover spirituality for yourself; make up your own mind. What do you have to lose?

Chapter 12: Universal Spiritual Truths

All truths are easy to understand once they are discovered; the point is to discover them.
– Galileo Galilei

Religion offers important spiritual truths. It is not necessary to be religious to understand these truths, and these truths are universal regardless of religious persuasion.

Spirituality, however, goes deeper than religion. Religion tells us what to expect and how to behave in order to have a spiritual experience with God. It can be compared to reading a menu in a fine restaurant, but it is never a substitute for experiencing the actual meal. A good menu offers a mouthwatering expectation of what is to come, it whets the appetite. The real experience, however, is in tasting and enjoying the food. Many people experience spirituality as a repeated faithful studying of the menu when in fact there is far more to experience. True spirituality is being touched by God in a supernatural way resulting in a life transforming experience.

Let's see what the menus from some of the major religions have to offer. The information presented here is offered as a summary only and in good faith to fairly represent the major religious views, and in so doing reveal important universal spiritual truths.

The Hindu faith

The Hindu faith is a complex religion that recognises a supreme deity called Brahman. Brahman the universal soul or the ultimate reality, and it is also recognised as Vishnu, Siva, Brahma or Shakti depending on the religious sect. The Hindus view the soul as indestructible, immortal and indistinct from Brahman. Through a process of *karma* (deeds and actions, the moral law of cause and effect) and *samsara* (a process of reaction; birth, death and rebirth or reincarnation) the soul eventually becomes "one with the universal soul". In so doing, the soul

TRUE SPIRITUALITY IS BEING TOUCHED BY GOD IN A SUPERNATURAL WAY RESULTING IN A LIFE TRANSFORMING EXPERIENCE.

experiences freedom from the cycle of life and death, and achieves ultimate enlightenment (*moksha*).

There are many manifestations of God (demi-gods or *devas*) in the Hindu faith, and Hindus worship their particular choice of god in order to achieve eventual enlightenment. Devas may be good or evil, and influence the course of life. Good deeds are rewarded, resulting in a greater enlightenment. Evil deeds pollute the believer's soul, taking it further away from the ecstatic joy of being one with the universal soul. The evil soul is punished at death by returning to life in a lower form at the next incarnation.

Buddhism

Buddhism is a religion based on the teachings of the Buddha. Buddha is not a god; rather, he was an enlightened person who showed the way of awakening or enlightenment.

Buddhism encourages enlightenment by studying the Dharma, leading a good life and purifying the mind. The final goal is to be rewarded by the end of suffering as the Buddhist attains the state of nirvana, a place or state characterised by freedom from pain, worry and the external world.

THE MAIN TENETS OF BUDDHISM ARE THAT GOODNESS IS REWARDED AND EVIL PUNISHED.

As with Hinduism, there is a belief in reincarnation. In this process, the spirit is continually reborn after death until ultimate enlightenment is achieved. Reincarnation can occur outside the realms of humanity, including the hells, animal kingdom, human world, the world of jealous gods and the heavens. The outcome of the next life is determined by *karma*, a tally sheet of good and bad deeds.

The main tenets of Buddhism are that goodness is rewarded and evil punished. Death reflects how life was lived. Seek well, reject evil and shed ignorance.

Islam

Islam (as well as Judaism and Christianity) recognises only one God. God is supreme, almighty and the one known as Allah. The Qur'an is believed to be the words of Allah spoken through the prophet Muhammad. The Muslim faith also recognises Adam, Noah, Abraham, Moses and Jesus as prophets. Muslims believe there will be no other prophets to follow Muhammad.

BELIEVING IN ALLAH AND LIVING A GOOD LIFE BY FULFILLING THE PILLARS OF THE MUSLIM FAITH WILL RESULT IN ETERNAL REWARD IN PARADISE AT THE LAST JUDGEMENT.

Islamic belief encompasses the concept of an all-powerful and almighty God, angels, God's messengers, God's revealed books, divine predestination and a final day of resurrection and judgement. Believing in Allah and living a good life by fulfilling the pillars of the Muslim faith will result in eternal reward in Paradise at the last judgement. Unbelievers and those who have been evil will have to face an eternal punishment in hell.

Unlike Hinduism and Buddhism, Islam does not allow for second chances by way of reincarnation. This life is lived in preparation for the eternal life to follow at the time of judgement.

The Jewish faith

The Jewish faith is a complex faith established on the Torah (the divine word of God) and the Talmud (the interpretation of the law). The Jewish faith recognises one God, the creator. God is omnipotent, almighty and supreme. He has established a special covenant pact with the Jewish nation through Abraham. God delivered his law (the Torah) through the prophet Moses. The Jewish faith recognises that God judges the deeds of man, that good will be rewarded and evil punished. Adherents to the faith believe in a revival of the dead.

THE JEWISH FAITH RECOGNISES ONE GOD, THE CREATOR. GOD IS OMNIPOTENT, ALMIGHTY AND SUPREME.

The concept of an afterlife is debated, but there appears to be evidence from the psalms that King David refers to Sheol, a place after death. The prophet Daniel is also told that he would rest at the end of his days, until the time of judgement.

The Jewish faith has an expectation of a Messiah, a supreme king who will rule the Jewish nation.

In Judaism, death is not a tragedy. Death is a natural process. Our deaths, like our lives, have meaning and are all part of God's plan. There is a world to come, where those who have lived a worthy life will be rewarded.

The Christian faith

The Christian faith, unlike the Jewish faith, believes that Jesus the Messiah (Christ) has come. The Christian faith is founded on a belief in God the Father, Jesus Christ as the Son of God and the Holy Spirit. Christians believe in the death, descent into hell, resurrection and ascension of Christ.

In Christianity, the Messiah's Second Coming will be a day of judgement and salvation for the faithful. Wickedness will be punished and the saved, who are those who have faith in Christ, will be rewarded at the final Judgement.

Universal spiritual truths

Religion, subject to varied interpretation and opinion, tries its best to define spirituality. Within its limitations, and re-gardless of religious persuasion, the following universal spiritual truths are apparent as they relate to an individual's understanding about God:

1. There is an ongoing existence of the human soul after death.
2. All souls are destined to eventually meet with God.

3. All souls have accountability – good deeds will be rewarded and evil deeds will be punished.

The believer's dilemma

Everyone is a believer; everyone has faith!

We all inherently believe in something. This core belief sets the course of each life, and it determines the philosophy by which we choose to live. This philosophy may be grounded in religion or cast in the stone of culture and tradition. The philosophy may be based on an intelligent appraisal of measurable facts. Or it may simply be an unwavering belief in self. Whether this core belief is well-developed or vague, it is very resistant to change.

> WE ALL INHERENTLY BELIEVE IN SOMETHING. THIS CORE BELIEF SETS THE COURSE OF EACH LIFE, AND IT DETERMINES THE PHILOSOPHY BY WHICH WE CHOOSE TO LIVE.

It is this constancy that gives rise to the believer's dilemma. If we dare to change our core belief, we change everything. It is easier to believe what is convenient and safe and comfortable than to ever consider changing that core belief.

The universal spiritual truths on which many religions are founded will not be part of everyone's core belief. These may, indeed, be very controversial beliefs for some people. Some may find it difficult to believe that we have an eternal soul, or find it too overwhelming to believe in the existence of God. These spiritual truths may simply be disregarded as religious propaganda.

What do you believe happens at death? Are you sure?

Perhaps death is not as terrible as it may seem? In a spiritual context, dying opens up the way to new exciting possibilities. Religious terms such as Paradise, Heaven, Nirvana and blissful enlightenment all try to convey the sublime pleasure that can be expected after death. The promise of eternal happiness is not to be ignored. Everyone is invited to participate in this eternal happiness. Don't let the opportunity pass because of entrenched core beliefs.

CONSIDER THE EXPERIENCES OF THOSE WHO HAVE DIED AND LIVED TO TELL THE TALE. THESE NEAR-DEATH EXPERIENCES OFFER AMAZING REVELATIONS ABOUT WHAT HAPPENS WHEN WE DIE.

This is not a call to be religious. It is a call to be open-minded about the possibility of life after death. Consider the experiences of those who have died and lived to tell the tale. These Near-Death Experiences offer amazing revelations about what happens when we die.

Chapter 13: Near-Death Experiences

We understand why children are afraid of darkness ... but why are men afraid of light?
– Plato

Death is usually regarded as an irreversible one-way event. People who have died do not have the option to return to life. Yet, remarkably, some people have died and returned to tell their amazing story. Their experiences are known as Near-Death Experiences (or NDEs for short).

Near-Death Experiences provide us with compelling evidence that there is life beyond the grave. Death is no more than a separation from an apparently very limited physical body and earthly experience. In dying, a new unfathomable dimension opens up. Those who have experienced NDEs are unable to find adequate words to describe their experience. They rely on exaggeration such as "a million times more wonderful" or "worse than a million garbage dumps" to describe their experience.

Whereas some people's NDEs are ecstatically wonderful, not all NDEs seem to be. Although the details vary, NDEs share a number of features.

A sense of being dead

Those people who have had an NDE know they have died. In addition, they all experienced a life-threatening event preceding their NDE, either by way of severe trauma or illness. The medical facts associated with their experience (when they are available) are in keeping with a clinical death. People experiencing an NDE are instantly released from the pain and suffering associated with their grave medical condition.

NEAR-DEATH EXPERIENCES PROVIDE US WITH COMPELLING EVIDENCE THAT THERE IS LIFE BEYOND THE GRAVE.

An "out of body" experience

Near-Death Experiences bring with them a sensation of the spirit or soul leaving the physical body in an "out-of-the-body" experience. People who have had NDEs often recount that, as their soul leaves the physical body, they have often become spectators to the drama associated with their death. They may, for example, be able to recall details of events associated with their resuscitation as medical teams desperately try and revive them. They witness the lifelessness of their body as the soul has departed, as if the power source of life has been cut off.

A journey to another dimension

Once the soul has left the body, it begins a journey to another reality or dimension. Those who have had NDEs are adamant that they are not dreaming but experiencing the vivid reality of the spiritual realm. This journey is often described as travelling down a passage or a tunnel of light. Some people describe a sense of having life events flash past them on this journey. The soul may be accompanied by angelic beings or the souls of past friends or relatives who have died.

THE SOUL MAY BE ACCOMPANIED BY ANGELIC BEINGS OR THE SOULS OF PAST FRIENDS OR RELATIVES WHO HAVE DIED.

Arrival at a boundary or destination

Often the journey ends with a sense of arriving at a place of great beauty. There is usually an experience of profound peace, happiness, joy and love. Some people have a meeting with Jesus or God, or an angel. They have an absolute desire to remain in this place forever. Many people who have had NDEs describe this place as Heaven.

But happiness does not seem to be destined for everyone. Some of those who have had NDEs describe the experience of travelling to a place of great darkness, fear and torment. They are escorted by what can be described as demons and underworld characters, and know that the final destination will be what they describe as Hell.

A call to return to the physical body

Some people remember being told that their time has not come and that they have to return to Earth to complete their life. Many feel great reluctance at having to leave the place of such splendour and happiness.

THOSE WHO HAVE HAD A POSITIVE NDE NO LONGER FEAR DEATH.

Those who have had a negative NDE are shaken and distressed by their experience. They are overwhelmed and thankful to be able to escape the horror of their NDE.

The return to the physical body is associated with a return to the suffering associated with the illness or trauma that preceded the NDE. Life returns to the body, and vital signs are restored.

A life-changing experience

Life can never be the same after an NDE.

Those who have had a positive NDE no longer fear death. In comparison to the abundant ecstasy of the other dimension, life on Earth becomes dull and unattractive. It takes a long time for them to settle back into ordinary life as they long to return to the place they encountered during their NDE.

Those who have had a negative experience also have a life-changing experience as they seek to find salvation for their souls.

Often those experiencing an NDE have to suffer the physical trauma associated with their injury and illness. It may take months to recover. In this process, there is often an ongoing association with the spiritual world. It is as if a veil has been lifted for a time, and those who have died can communicate freely with the spiritual world for a while. With time, the dullness and darkness of this world cloud the veil. The link to the spiritual dimension closes, leaving a lingering hope of returning to Paradise in the time to come.

THE LINK TO THE SPIRITUAL DIMENSION CLOSES, LEAVING A LINGERING HOPE OF RETURNING TO PARADISE IN THE TIME TO COME.

The concept of Near-Death Experiences is not universally recognised. Scientific opinion is that the NDE is no more than the final "spasm" of a dying brain. Many medical professionals believe that NDEs occur as the body dies, as a result of terminal electric impulses in the oxygen-starved brain. Others, however, argue that those who have had an NDE quite often have a remarkable recollection and consciousness of the dramatic events surrounding their death experience. One person reported being able to clearly recall the events and the name of the nurse who removed his false teeth during his out-of-body experience and unconsciousness associated with his NDE.

Eben Alexander describes his NDE experience in his book *Proof of Heaven: A Neurosurgeon's Journey into the Afterlife* (2012). As a neurosurgeon, knowledgeable in the function of the brain, Alexander refutes the argument that an NDE is no more than electrical impulses in a dying brain. Rather than unconsciousness, his recollection in dying was of a vastly increased consciousness. Alexander says the following about his experience:

> But conveying that knowledge now is rather like being a chimpanzee, becoming a human for a single day to experience all the wonders of human knowledge, and then returning to one's chimp friends and trying to tell them what it was like knowing several different Romance languages, the calculus and the immense scale of the universe.

There are many other accounts of NDEs. The following are some of my favourites.

George Foreman's NDE

George Foreman, the famous boxer and former World Heavyweight Champion, had his NDE after losing a boxing match to Jimmy Young in Puerto Rico in 1977. It was a life-transforming event. Foreman recounts his experience in his memoir *God in My Corner: A Spiritual Memoir* (2007).

> I knew I was dead and this wasn't Heaven. I was terrified, knowing I had no way out. Sorrow beyond description engulfed my soul, more than anyone could ever imagine. If you multiplied every disturbing and frightening thought that you've ever had during your entire life, that wouldn't come close to the panic I felt.

Foreman goes on to describe how he cried out to God and how he was rescued.

> Instantly what seemed like a gigantic hand reached down and snatched me out of the terrifying place. Immediately I was back inside my body in the dressing room. I couldn't believe it; I wasn't in darkness anymore! Even though I lost all hope of escaping, God had mercifully let me out!

Transformed from a non-religious, unbelieving person to someone with a profound faith in Jesus, Foreman's account of his NDE and the reality of the goodness resulting from his experience is a dramatic one.

Mary C. Neal's NDE

In her book *To Heaven and Back* (2012), Dr Mary C. Neal, an orthopaedic surgeon, describes her NDE. Sucked underwater in a white-water kayaking accident in Chile, Mary died and went to Heaven. Her description of the event follows:

> It felt as if I had finally shaken off my heavy outer layer, freeing my soul. I rose up out of the river, and when my soul broke through the surface of the water, I encountered a group of fifteen to twenty souls (human spirits sent from God), who greeted me with the most overwhelming joy I have ever experienced and could ever imagine.

Neal goes on to recount her experience as she travelled to Heaven. She had a consciousness about what was happening to her lifeless body:

> My body looked like the shell of a comfortable old friend, and I felt a warm compassion and gratitude for its use.

> I looked at Tom and his sons and they seemed terribly sad and vulnerable. I heard them call to me and beg me to take a breath. I loved them and did not want them to be sad, so I asked my Heavenly companions to wait while I returned to my body, lay down and took a

breath. Thinking this would be satisfactory I then left my body and resumed my journey home.

Neal reflects that in dying we are returning home. I imagine that this must be with the same joy and enthusiasm a child experiences in returning to his home after a time away. Home, in the best sense, is a place of safety and love and acceptance. It is where we ultimately belong.

Death, then, may not be a sad eternal separation but rather a homecoming. It is potentially a time of unbridled joy as we are united with loved ones and God. Dying is no more than a transition into a new dimension, one where the physical body may not come.

DYING IS NO MORE THAN A TRANSITION INTO A NEW DIMENSION, ONE WHERE THE PHYSICAL BODY MAY NOT COME.

The essence of each person is the soul or spirit. It endures forever. If we spend so much time and effort caring for the physical body that is destined to perish and fade away, how much more should we care for the spirit within us?

Chapter 14:
The Spirit* Within

It is only to the individual that a soul is given.
– Albert Einstein

*The term soul and spirit are used interchangeably and for the purpose of clarity they are not defined beyond being the immortal essence of a person.

We assume the existence of many things we cannot see. We cannot see the wind, but we can see the effects of the wind as trees sway in the breeze, or the aftermath of the wind following a tropical cyclone. We know about oxygen and its importance to life yet we cannot actually see it. The visible spectrum of light only illuminates a very narrow portion of the electromagnetic spectrum. Most things are unseen. We believe they exist either by inferred scientific method or because we have been told they exist.

In the spiritual dimension, things are invisible unless, occasionally, they are revealed for a purpose and a reason. Spiritual knowledge is not measurable, but it has been recorded. Often, accounts of spirituality are deemed to be miraculous because they defy the natural norm and standard. Spirituality cannot easily be assessed by scientific method, and because of this we have to rely on the stories that have been revealed and told.

THE VISIBLE SPECTRUM OF LIGHT ONLY ILLUMINATES A VERY NARROW PORTION OF THE ELECTROMAGNETIC SPECTRUM. MOST THINGS ARE UNSEEN.

Sacred religious teaching, ancient traditions and recorded personal testimony are the framework for discovering spirituality. It is an active process of discovery. It is a personal journey that cannot be delegated. It is an experience that cannot be bought. It comes down to a personal choice, and this choice affects the welfare of the soul or spirit within each one of us.

The soul is the immortal essence of a person. It is hidden deep within. It has no dimension; it is invisible and ill-defined. The soul is often described as the heart or psyche of a person. If you were to point to a region of your body in which the soul might be found it would not be the head, but rather the place of deepest emotion somewhere in the belly or lower chest. It is that core part of us that defines who we really are when all pretence is removed. It is that part that remains when the external wrapping of the physical body is gone.

Each person has a soul and each soul has similar attributes.

The soul is immortal

The soul can never die. It is eternal. It is the indestructible, permanent you. As such, you never end, but continue to exist forever.

The character of the soul is shaped in life

At birth, the soul is as a batch of new potting clay – it is untouched and ready to be formed in life. Each experience and each choice shapes the clay. Some experiences are bitter and tragic, while others are fantastic and memorable. In the journey through life the soul can become battered and bruised. It may be so neglected it is as if it doesn't exist. The soul exists in the spiritual dimension, and as such, is subject to spiritual influences.

THE SOUL IS THE IMMORTAL ESSENCE OF A PERSON. IT IS HIDDEN DEEP WITHIN. IT HAS NO DIMENSION; IT IS INVISIBLE AND ILL-DEFINED.

The soul is recognisable after death

In reviewing near-death experiences, it is apparent that parents, grandparents and friends known in life are recognisable in the afterlife. Although the physical body no longer exists, the character of the soul remains readily identifiable. The soul does not require a nametag after death.

The soul is priceless

The soul is priceless and cannot be compared to any of life's treasures. Life choices are frequently based on financial rewards and immediate gratification yet these are of no enduring value. Choices affecting the character of the soul are of eternal value. If the soul was worth a miserable dollar a day, its value would quickly add up in the realm of eternity. Most people don't realize how valuable they are.

The soul is accountable

The soul is accountable for the way in which life was lived. Good deeds are ultimately rewarded. The terms Nirvana, Paradise or Heaven are used to express the reward of ultimate happiness and joy. Evil deeds are not left unpunished.

The soul returns to God

After death, the soul that has been liberated from the lifeless body ultimately returns to God. God is the final destination. It is beneficial to know God on this side of life so that it is not an awkward encounter.

The soul has free choice

Regardless of the experience, it is ultimately the choice between good and evil that determines the eventual character of the soul. Good people choose to do good even in tough times. The choices you make today have an effect on the character of the soul. Each soul has the freedom to choose its spiritual path and also to change the path if it so chooses. The destiny of each soul lies in each individual's hands.

As such, the welfare of our soul is our responsibility. It is our greatest asset. It cannot be ignored, and if it has not been nurtured, it requires urgent attention.

After being born, we feed the body, providing it with nutrition. We cleanse the body to keep healthy and presentable. We exercise the body to allow it to be able to perform its functions adequately. A healthy, physical body is a gift, one we appreciate more and more as we age.

> EACH SOUL HAS THE FREEDOM TO CHOOSE ITS SPIRITUAL PATH AND ALSO TO CHANGE THE PATH IF IT SO CHOOSES.

The spirit within us also requires attention. Mostly it is dormant and passive, subject to the spiritual forces that influence it in life. Once awakened, the spirit becomes a dynamo for life. It changes from being a bystander to actively participating in the purpose of life.

As with the body, the spirit requires nutrition, cleansing and exercise to survive in the spiritual world. Spiritual awakening begins with seeking. It requires a hunger to know more about God. Spiritual nutrition comes from reading the sacred writings and teachings. Spiritual cleansing ultimately comes from God, and spiritual fitness from prayer and meditation.

Taken together, these disciplines offer great benefit to the soul.

The key to spiritual well-being, however, is not so much about what we do, but what God has done. Many people seek spiritual enlightenment by striving for perfection

ONCE AWAKENED, THE SPIRIT BECOMES A DYNAMO FOR LIFE.

when in truth perfection comes from knowing God. The ultimate destination of each soul is God, and finding the right God is the answer to eternal happiness.

Chapter 15: Finding God

Never be afraid to trust an
unknown future to a known God.
– Corrie Ten Boom

Seeking God is no easy task. It is not as if God is clearly visible and easy to find. In the confusion of religion and amongst the millions of so-called gods, where can the ultimate truth be found? If you asked a Hindu about God, he or she may name one of a handful of favourites in a list of millions of possible gods. The Christians would describe Jehovah and the Muslims would demand Allah. And some would say there is no God.

What do you think?

Before considering God, it is important to consider religion and get it out the way. Religion offers a conscious physical view of the invisible spiritual dimension. As such, it has limitations. The messages given to nourish the soul often turn into a list of regulations open to interpretation and debate. Ultimately, this leads to conflict because someone has to be right or wrong. Religion leads to exclusivity as opposed to the true spiritual message, which is an invitation for all people to know God.

IN THE CONFUSION OF RELIGION AND AMONGST THE MILLIONS OF SO-CALLED GODS, WHERE CAN THE ULTIMATE TRUTH BE FOUND?

Spirituality is deeper than religion. It assumes nothing and depends on God. At the heart of spirituality is trust and humility. In this invisible, immeasurable dimension, we need to trust something. It is easier to trust God than to trust the interpretation of spirituality given by a priest, an imam or a rabbi, or anyone else for that matter.

To trust God, it is important to first know about God. For those who don't have a god the decision is easy. They trust in themselves or in the provision of a social political system. They, in essence, become their own god, determining their own course in life. They maintain independence, but they are not independent. The invisible spiritual world remains real and it affects the character of their soul.

For those who do have a god, the choice is more complex. Is your god living up to his reputation? Gods, in general, demand sacrifice, obedience, and homage. They punish offenders and they are intolerant of wrongdoing. Gods are not always kind. It is dangerous to mess with God. Don't go picking a fight with the wrong god. How well do you know your God?

SPIRITUALITY IS DEEPER THAN RELIGION.

There is a god who describes Himself as the God of love. He is personal and has a name, preferring the name *Father* as he views us as his children. He demands sacrifice and *He* provides the sacrifice. He desires obedience and offers His spirit to help and comfort us towards achieving this goal. He desires worship because it is liberating to worship this great God. He tolerates offenders, showing mercy rather than meting out punishment for offences. He knows the human heart as He became human. This God is kind and patient. He is not rude or boastful.

EACH SOUL IS DESTINED FOR AN ENCOUNTER WITH GOD. IT IS A GOOD WAY TO END EACH STORY.

There is no fear with this God. The benefits of knowing Him are that He gives peace and joy to His children.

Are you at peace? Has your soul found rest?

Each soul is destined for an encounter with God. It is a good way to end each story. I can think of no better way. But the story is not over yet and there is still a whole lot of living to do.

Chapter 16: Getting On With Life

Get busy living or get busy dying.
— Stephen King, *Different Seasons*

In the mad rush to succeed, create wealth or simply keep up with the Joneses some things are often left behind and neglected. If your life has been anything like my life, it is rush, rush to get through school and on to university. Then it's full steam ahead to obtain a degree and a further degree, and suddenly ten years have gone by. Get a good job, brimming with professional pride; marriage and kids follow. Then it's back to the mad rush-rush to get the children to the best schools, for the best universities and the best jobs.

Whoa! Slow down a bit. Is this what life is all about, a mad hamster wheel spinning around at ever increasing speeds so that we can keep up with all the other hamsters spinning around on their wheels? Often, it takes misfortune, such as illness, to bump us off this crazy ride.

If you had enough money not to ever have to work again, what would you do? What are your passions and the things in life that you would like to pursue? Sadly, we have to work for a living, but that's just it, we have to live. Living is more than working. The bigger house and bigger car and bigger mortgage don't add to life – they add to the complexity in life. Ask someone facing an incurable illness about how important the new European car is if you want a more real perspective on what's really important in life.

FRIENDSHIPS HAVE ETERNAL VALUE. KEEP A SHORT RECORD OF WRONGS, AND ALLOW TIME AND SPACE FOR RECONCILIATION.

Relationships are important. Having a happy marriage and children that speak to you and visit regularly is important. Having grandchildren that care about you is important. If these things have been neglected, start paying attention. Friendships have eternal value. Keep a short record of wrongs, and allow time and space for reconciliation. Maintaining or restoring relationships takes effort and commitment. Start by writing a letter or by simply telling someone you care about that you love them.

Solitude is important. Take time out away from the rat race and the never-ending chores of everyday life. Find a place where it is just you and spend some time in your own company. How well do you know yourself? What kind of person are you? What do your friends say about you? What do you say about yourself? Some people live a lifetime without really knowing who they are. Discover who you are. Then discover who *you can be* even if it seems that time is against you.

Kindness is important. Start by being kind to yourself. Be friendly to the person looking back at you in the mirror every day. Consider thanking them for putting up with you all these years. As crazy as it sounds, many of us forget that we are our own best friend. Show it to yourself and then show it to others. Be generous. Give freely, not expecting anything back in return, because that defines true giving. Make someone else's day great if you cannot have a great day.

DISCOVER WHO YOU ARE. THEN DISCOVER WHO YOU CAN BE EVEN IF IT SEEMS THAT TIME IS AGAINST YOU.

Thankfulness is important. Be thankful for small things: the fresh breeze on a hot day, the fragrance of a flower, the distant laughter of a child. Stop to see the world in slow motion .The great song by "Satchmo" Louis Armstrong, "What a Wonderful World", embraces this attitude of thankfulness. Enjoy the wonder of this world.

Make a list of things you want to experience in life. In the movie *The Bucket List,* Edward and Carter set out on a journey of discovery when they discover they have limited time after being diagnosed with incurable lung cancer. What are the things you still *have* to do in life? They may not seem achievable, but with friends and community support it may be possible to do that "one thing" you have always wanted to do, be it a skydive, snorkelling the Great Barrier Reef, seeing the Pyramids or riding an elephant.

YOU DON'T HAVE TO HAVE A TERMINAL ILLNESS TO HAVE A "BUCKET LIST". MAKE A LIST OF THE THINGS YOU WANT TO DO.

You don't have to have a terminal illness to have a "bucket list". Make a list of the things *you* want to do. Add to it or remove those things that are no longer important. It is your list, so be bold. There are so many great things to do in life – the sooner you start, the greater your chance of completing the list. One friend's son always wanted to do all the great rollercoaster rides in the USA. He did it after school. Tick, one item done! What's on your list?

It may be something dramatic, such as saving the planet or the whales, or going on a religious pilgrimage, or volunteering to work in a refugee camp. Or it may simply be to go fishing. Whatever you decide to do is great, but there are a few things that should be on everyone's list of things to do and some of these are covered in the following chapter.

Chapter 17: Essential Things to Do Before You Die

You may delay, but time will not.
– Benjamin Franklin

There are some things that must be done in life. Leaving them unattended is not necessarily criminal, but it may be a close call. Getting dressed, feeding the pets, paying bills and doing taxes are all everyday chores that must be done. If they are left unattended – particularly the getting dressed part of the day – there will be consequences and they won't be pleasant.

When it comes to dying, there are also things to which you must attend. If you speak to people in the legal or insurance fields they will tell you tale after tale about misfortune that occurred because people were not prepared for the events that occur after death. Untold sadness, frustration and borderline criminal anger follow if some essentials are not attended to before death.

Here is my list of essential things to do before you die.

Draw up a will
"Where the dead are, the vultures will gather."

You can be sure that if you have *any* assets, some people will be interested in your demise. This is particularly so if you have great wealth. As cynical as this may sound, it is often the sad truth if a will has not been drafted.

A WILL SHOULD GIVE CLEAR INSTRUCTION ABOUT THE DISPOSAL OF YOUR ASSETS WHEN YOU ARE DEAD AND NO LONGER ABLE TO MAKE ANY COMMENT.

A will should give clear instruction about the disposal of your assets when you are dead and no longer able to make any comment. Ambiguous statements are open to interpretation, creating fertile ground for misunderstanding, conflict and general unhappiness in some way or other. It is also fertile soil for lawyers who have to unravel the ambiguities at great cost. Preparation saves time and money.

Circumstances in life change and a will must reflect these changes. A friend recently died with an out-dated will. The will failed to recognise that he had separated from his wife and that the assets had already been fairly shared. Because his will reflected his views in a previous era, when things were different, his estranged wife had the legal right to all his remaining assets. The fairness of this can be debated, but in the end it does not matter because the will is binding.

Don't leave everyone guessing. Update your will regularly. Get legal advice. Pay that extra dollar for sound advice and get a comprehensive product without ambiguities. See it as an investment in your legacy.

Seek financial advice about estate planning

One of the interested parties lurking around after you die is the taxman. Death taxes are a fantastic source of funding for any government. After all, you won't be there to object!

Estate planning allows for legal strategies to minimise the effects of tax. It may mean distributing some of your assets earlier on or into a trust. Each circumstance is unique – find out what is best for you by speaking to your accountant or financial advisor.

Why leave the tax department with an unfair portion of your hard-earned money?

Consider an advanced directive

An advanced directive is an essential document that provides clear instructions about how you want to be cared for when you are no longer able to make the decision for yourself.

It details whether you do (or don't) want to be resuscitated and placed on a ventilator, if you suffered a massive stroke, for example. It gives your carers clear instructions about how to manage your health when you cannot.

Medical care is committed to saving life even when it is futile. Against all hope and at enormous cost the medical establishment will continue to try to save life until courts decide if life should continue. An advanced directive helps make the decision clearer.

Discuss advanced directives with your carers and doctors.

Do funeral planning

Who wants to have a miserable funeral? Make your funeral one with a difference. Decide whom you would like to do the eulogy. Decide where you want to be buried, or if you are cremated, where you would like the ashes to end up.

FUNERALS NO LONGER HAVE TO BE ANGUISHING OUTPOURINGS OF GRIEF. THEY ARE ALLOWED TO BE A CELEBRATION OF LIFE.

Funerals no longer have to be anguishing outpourings of grief. They are allowed to be a celebration of life. Be the life of the party, even if you cannot be there in person.

Discuss the modern exciting options for a funeral with a modern funeral director. Think about a "green" funeral or about having a brightly coloured casket. Funerals have changed so much, so why not do something new?

Find a palliative care service

In the setting of progressive incurable illness, find a good palliative care team early on. Many people confuse palliative care with terminal care. Palliative care begins much earlier, and yes, it does eventually involve terminal care.

> GOOD PALLIATIVE CARE AFFIRMS LIFE, ALLOWING EACH INDIVIDUAL TO LIVE LIFE TO ITS BEST UNTIL LIFE IS NO LONGER POSSIBLE.

In the weeks and months leading up to death, more resources are required in daily care. Getting the right team on board and knowing the team and what they have to offer reduces much of the distress associated with dying. Good palliative care affirms life, allowing each individual to live life to its best until life is no longer possible.

Find a doctor you can trust and be comfortable with. I have found that the palliative care teams and hospices have some of the most compassionate people around. Make use of their specialised skills when you need them.

Write

Don't leave without having a final word. Your life is a treasure of experiences and ideas, memories and sage words of

> YOU HAVE LIVED LIFE SO TAKE TIME TO RECORD IT. FIND A JOURNAL, PREFERABLY ONE THAT PROMPTS YOU, AND WRITE DOWN THE THINGS THAT MATTER.

advice. You have lived life so take time to record it. Find a journal, preferably one that prompts you, and write down the things that matter.

It may seem trivial at first, but the history of where you were born, what the town looked like and who you went to school with will be a precious memory for someone. Your grandchildren and great-grandchildren will be able to identify with these events when you come up in conversation. The more you write, the more they can enjoy your life even when you are gone.

Write a letter to those you care about. Explain why they matter to you. They will treasure the personal touch, particularly if it is left for them after you have died.

Do a professional photo shoot

With the widespread use of digital cameras on almost every device, there is no lack of photos to be had. Unfortunately, these are not necessarily the greatest artistic creations. They are good for every day, but we all need a special day.

Attending a professional photo shoot may sound like a lot of hard work and an unwanted expense, but the end product –

you – will be worth it. Spoil yourself and your family by doing this outrageous activity regularly.

Professional photos don't need to be studio photos or those boring photos seen on the living room wall. They can be as informal as you like, or even action shots. The essence is the quality of the photo, capturing that moment in your life when you are at ease and happy and the way you want to be seen and remembered.

Say a prayer and make peace with God

Perhaps you have never said a prayer in your life and are not sure where to begin. Begin by imagining that there is a God that cares to listen and tell Him what's on your heart. Be honest, say what you will and then follow your heart.

BE HONEST. CONFIDE IN GOD AS YOU WOULD A CLOSE FRIEND.

Prayer is a two-way conversation, and if you start, I expect that God will answer you. It may be in an unexpected way, it may be at an unexpected time, but He will answer. He always does when prayer comes from the heart.

If you do pray regularly and have never heard back from God, change the way you pray. Forget the religion and the things you have been taught. Be honest. Confide in God as you would a close friend.

Here is an example of a simple prayer:

> *"I pray to the living God, the only true God.*
> *Please hear me and allow me to hear from you.*
> *Forgive darkness in my life and show me your*
> *light.*
> *These are the things that are on my heart..."*

Forgive

We all make mistakes. We all do stupid things at times. One of these things is not to forgive.

Sometimes people bear a grudge their whole life. It is hard work bearing a permanent grudge; it takes effort to continually remind oneself of past insult and play it over and over in the mind. If you feel aggrieved about a past wrong, I am sure the offence must have been worth it, but let it go. Let bygones be bygones. Let the grudge die before you die.

FORGIVENESS IS LIBERATING. DON'T FORGET TO FORGIVE YOURSELF.

Forgiveness is liberating.

Don't forget to forgive yourself.

Give

I spoke to a man in his last few weeks of life who mentioned that he had nothing to live for. Nothing gave him any pleasure anymore. He had no joy in reading or watching television or listening to music. His life was ending and he was missing a golden opportunity to make a real difference in this life.

We live this life only once, and we have an opportunity to do something good. Giving is something good! It should not be out of duty or forced. It should not be based on guilt. It should not be out of pity.

Giving should be from a thankful heart, one that recognises that in life we have often received a gift and that in receiving a gift we have been blessed. Giving is about wanting to share a blessing with someone else.

> GIVING IS ABOUT WANTING TO SHARE A BLESSING WITH SOMEONE ELSE.

Perhaps dying is an opportunity to consider that you can make a *real difference* in the life of someone else. They will never know who you are, they will never be able to thank you or shake your hand in gratitude, but they will be blessed. Their experience in this life may be changed forever by your action.

Make every moment count

We are all given twenty-four hours of opportunity every day. Make each day count. Don't be caught in the deception that life is about acquiring wealth, for which we must all work harder for longer. Stop and smell the proverbial roses! Take time to enjoy the laughter of children, to see the splendour of sunsets, to smell the musty soil in a dense forest and to let the surf break relentlessly on your tanned body.

Life is a gift to enjoy. Make sure that you enjoy something each day and share it with someone else.

Chapter 18: The End

The end of life is to be like God, and the soul following God will be like Him.

– Socrates

There are no professionals in the act of dying. What I mean by this is that no-one has done it before and repeated it with sufficient practice to be able to say "Hey, this is the way it's to be done". We each get one go. As such, we are all amateurs when it comes to dying. We may see others die and go before us, but there is no certainty that they got it right or wrong.

When the time comes to die, it is worth considering that it will be okay. Death is a natural everyday event. It happens to thousands of people daily, and has already happened to the millions who have gone before us. We certainly join the

> DEATH CANNOT BE AVOIDED. WHEN THE TIME COMES, ALLOW IT TO HAPPEN.

majority at death. At the time of death, events are beyond our control. Death cannot be avoided. When the time comes, allow it to happen.

I believe that death is not the end of our existence. Physically, it is an inconvenience and an unpleasant event that must pass. But it will pass and it will end and then…

Well, then it is really up to you!

The Christian faith offers enormous hope in the face of death. While most religions leave a person anguishing about the trade-off between good and evil, and getting it right and not wrong, the Christian faith simply states that *no one* gets it right. No amount of effort or hard work or practice at being good meets God's perfect standard. We all fail, each one of us. There are no saints, and as such, God needed to intervene.

The Christian message is centred on the love of God for us as humanity and on the person Jesus. As God, Jesus lived a perfect life and this perfect life is exchanged for our imperfect life. This divine exchange makes

> AS GOD, JESUS LIVED A PERFECT LIFE AND THIS PERFECT LIFE IS EXCHANGED FOR OUR IMPERFECT LIFE. THIS DIVINE EXCHANGE MAKES US ACCEPTABLE TO GOD.

us acceptable to God. There is no barrier that can separate us from the love of God. This is a simple message of eternal hope. Trust God and then follow Him in a new relationship.

> *"Whosoever shall call on the name of the Lord shall be saved"* (Acts 2:21).

Can it be any easier to make peace with God?

As an amateur, I have no real authority to make *any* comments about dying. My intention has been to normalise death, to say it's okay to die and to offer a hope beyond physical death. When my time comes to die, I too will tremble with the fear of uncertainty. I will be anguished as all those who have died before me. I will suffer the grief of having to say goodbye to the ones I love and the life I leave behind. But I will have courage based on my hope of life after death. I hope that when your time comes, you will be prepared for the passing event. I hope that you too may have a hope of life after death, and who knows, perhaps I may meet you in Paradise.

> WHEN MY TIME COMES TO DIE, I TOO WILL TREMBLE WITH THE FEAR OF UNCERTAINTY. I WILL BE ANGUISHED AS ALL THOSE WHO HAVE DIED BEFORE ME. I WILL SUFFER THE GRIEF OF HAVING TO SAY GOODBYE TO THE ONES I LOVE AND THE LIFE I LEAVE BEHIND.

About the Author

Colin was born in South Africa and grew up in the small mining town of Orkney. He attended St Stithians College in Johannesburg and from there went on to study medicine at the University of Pretoria. After graduating, Colin spent time in the United Kingdom before returning to South Africa to specialise in radiation oncology at the University of Pretoria.

Colin's restlessness and sense of adventure took him to New Zealand, where he completed his FRANZCR examination, as well as a diploma in palliative care via Cardiff University. He briefly returned to South Africa before finally settling on the Sunshine Coast of Australia, where he now resides.

As a radiation oncologist, working with cancer, Colin often has to initiate discussions about end-of-life care, death and dying. He believes that dialogue around the subject of dying is important, and that there is a great need to present information in a practical, compassionate and non-threatening manner. Colin developed the website www.dyingtounderstand.com to increase people's understanding and dispel unfounded myths about death and dying. His hope is to help others normalize the process of dying so that they can get on with living.

www.ingramcontent.com/pod-product-compliance
Lightning Source LLC
Chambersburg PA
CBHW060304050426
42448CB00009B/1741